The Authors

Lesley Faull was made *Commandeur Associé de la Commanderie des Cordons Bleus de France* in 1966. Today she is President of the Order in the Southern Hemisphere, and Silwood Kitchen – which she opened in 1963 – is now a *Cordon Bleu* school attended by students (including chefs) from all parts of Southern Africa. This book, dealing with the foods of yesterday, today and tomorrow, is a follower to *Cookery in Southern Africa Traditional and Today* (at the time of writing out of print), and was written in collaboration with co-author Vida Heard. Born in Natal, Lesley Faull is the daughter of the late Mr A. V. Allan, a pioneer of the dairy industry. When she married Dr George Faull and began to bring up a family of five children at Rondebosch, Cape, she took up cookery as a hobby; then, while studying every facet of the culinary arts including the "testing" of recipes, she started sharing her knowledge with housewives and manufacturers alike. A list of Mrs Faull's books appears on the inside of the back end paper of this book.

*　　*　　*

Vida Heard, journalist, was born in London and educated there and on the Continent. In this book, written in collaboration with Lesley Faull, she draws on her experience of housekeeping in half a dozen countries and also much cookery lore gleaned when she edited, in the early days, *The Homestead* (Supplement to the *Farmer's Weekly*) and, later on, *Femina and Woman's Life,* among other magazines. When she retired to Cape Town and met Lesley Faull her imagination was fired by Mrs Faull's plans to convert the old coach-house in the grounds of her home at Rondebosch into "a Mecca for cooking in Southern Africa", and she helped with publicity and the introduction of sponsors for Silwood Kitchen. With the same enthusiasm she has undertaken the research, writing and editing of her second historic cookery book.

Our Best Traditional Recipes

VIDA HEARD

AND

LESLEY FAULL

*Commandeur Associé
de la
Commanderie des Cordons Bleus de France*

Illustrated by Brenda Lighton

HOWARD TIMMINS

1975

Howard Timmins
45 Shortmarket Street
Cape Town

ISBN   0 86978 105 7

Printed by Galvin & Sales, Cape Town

Contents

Silwood Kitchen, at Rondebosch, Cape.

Acknowledgements

Silwood Kitchen has so many dear friends it is impossible for us to thank all from whom we draw information, inspiration and encouragement; and that includes our sponsors. But our special thanks must be recorded here for permission to quote Hildagonda Duckitt's recipes from her great-grand niece, Mrs Mary Kuttel. Then we'll never forget the help given us with our first historical book by Dr Mary Cook, of the Drostdy Museum, Swellendam, the late Lawrence Green, Mrs du Toit (V. M. FitzRoy), Mr and Mrs E. Schroeder (Malay customs) and many others which naturally flow into this our second "traditional" book. Lastly, but most important, is our appreciation of the fine artwork of our illustrator, Brenda Lighton, who originated this cover and did all the illustrations. Our sincere thanks, too, to Mr Howard Timmins for making this publication possible.

Lesley Faull
Vida Heard
March, 1975

A Handful of Metric for Good Measure
. . . and a pinch from the past

"A handful of this and a pinch of that" measured the recipes of our great-grannies and their "greats" before them.

Often today old-timers, and those not so old either, wish recipes could be as simple. But gradually we are all "buying" metric and the time is near – especially when today's school children qualify – when none of us will turn a hair at 250 ml or 500 g in a recipe. After all 250 ml *is* one measuring cup, approximating happily to our old American measuring cup of 8 fluid ounces – but *not* the Imperial (British) cup of 10 fluid ounces. Actually you'll find the new metric cup measures often show 300 ml – which makes it easy if you are converting from an English recipe because 300 ml is 10 oz.

500 g (which varies from 450 g to the larger figure) is our country's easy approximate conversion to 1 lb. But it should be remembered it is more than the former lb. (In Britain they metricise 16 oz = 450 g.)

We confess we are a bit worried by the new tablespoon of 12 .5 ml – which is a little less than the former tablespoon, but no one worries about the total banning of the dessertspoon. The teaspoon is near the old one, namely 5 ml. The new metric measures, as illustrated, are actually even easier to use than the old measures.

But Why Ml at all?

Well why not? Even our great-grans had to forego their "handfuls of this and pinches of that" for the Imperial pint and pound. Now all we are asked to do is to become part of the international metric system. So don't let's fight it, let's slide into it gracefully . . . as we have tried to do when converting these old recipes. And if some of you may criticise us for our bias towards South African metric measures our excuse is that this book, although intended also for world readership, is printed in South Africa – our only compromise being the decimal point instead of that very confusing comma when applied to cookery.

Special Note. When cup is mentioned in our recipes we refer to the standard cup of 250 ml (fortunately the same as our former South African (American) cup of 8 fluid ounces. When teaspoon and tablespoon are mentioned they refer to the 5 ml and 12 .5 ml respectively as shown in the illustrations and explained by the captions of our metric measuring utensils.

* * *

CHEF'S SECRET. Most of Silwood Kitchen's meat and savoury dishes are enhanced in flavour by the judicial use of MSG (monosodium glutamate) sold under various brand names including Zeal, Knorr Aromat, etc. Some commercial condiments contain MSG as an ingredient. Originally discovered by Chinese cooks centuries ago this cereal-derived product should not be confused with tenderizers and or food flavourings. It should be sprinkled over meats while cooking but not instead of salt or seasonings.

Metric Measuring Utensils

The following comprise the measuring utensils as approved by the South African Bureau of Standards:

A transparent cup of plastic or oven-proof glass marked in 10 ml divisions from 50 ml to 250 ml (and in some cases to 300 ml). It should be remembered that one South African cup is 250 ml – no more.

Above are measures for dry ingredients. A set of four plastic or metal measures when brimful measure 25 ml, 50 ml, 100 ml and 250 ml. Note that the largest, brimful, is exactly one cup, namely 250 ml.

This set of four plastic or metal spoons when brimful measure 1 ml, 2 ml, 5 ml and 12,5 ml. An extra 10 ml spoon may be introduced. Unfortunately the 12,5 ml spoon is slightly less than our former tablespoon, which is 15 ml.

A $^1/_4$ cup can be obtained by using the 50 ml measure plus the 12,5 ml spoon measure. If half a cup is required use the 100 ml measure, adding the 12,5 ml spoon measure twice.

Note: When measuring dry ingredients level measurements (not heaped) should be used.

How to Use Metric Measures

To measure liquids, convert from pints and quarts to millilitres and litres. Since 1927 South African recipes have been based on the American cup of 8 fluid ounces, while the British cup was larger, namely 10 fluid ounces. Now the new South African cup measure of 250 millilitres should be followed. Four cups can be used for measuing a litre. (Two pints, or one quart, are a little over a litre – 1,25 litres.) Using the new metric utensils, as illustrated, the following conversions are possible.

1/4 teaspoon	1 ml	2 teaspoons	10 ml
1/2 teaspoon	2 .5 ml	1 tablespoon	15 ml
1 teaspoon	5 ml	2 tablespoons	30 ml
1/4 cup	60 ml	1 cup	250 ml
1/3 cup	80 ml	2 cups	500 ml
1/2 cup	125 ml	3 cups	750 ml
3/4 cup	190 ml	4 cups (1 litre)	1 000 ml

Mass (Solids)

1 ounce	30 g	4 ounces	125 g
2 ounces	60 g	8 ounces	250 g
1 pound	500 g	6 pounds	3 kg
2 pounds	1 kg	7 pounds	3,5 kg
3 pounds	1,5 kg	8 pounds	4 kg
4 pounds	2 kg	9 pounds	4,5 kg
5 pounds	2,5 kg	10 pounds	5 kg

Temperature Equivalents

For those with stoves marked only in degrees Fahrenheit here are the following conversions to Celsius.

°C	°F	°C	°F
100	200	200	400
120	250	220	425
140	275	240	475
160	325	260	500
180	350	280	550

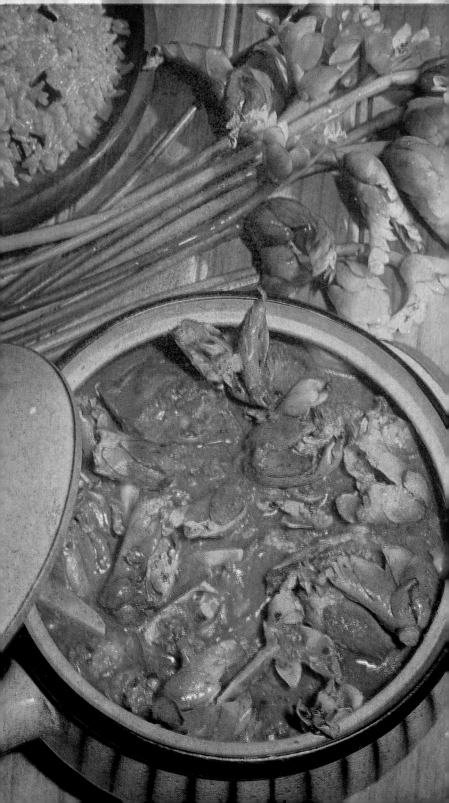

Introduction

As we Were . . . are . . . and May Be

This book is dedicated to the young and the old, those of both generations who enjoy savouring food spiced with a whiff of history.

Of course, to many older people, nothing does taste quite like it used to do, and for very good reason. Not only are taste buds (and teeth) older but foods are different. Fresh milk from the cow, unpasteurised, and poultry, non-battery, did contribute a special flavour, if not extra nutriment, to dishes.

In the old days every farmer's wife, many housewives and all bakers, for that matter, had their own special type of yeast, giving breads a variety of flavours. Some of these yeasts are included in these pages, as they are easily and cheaply made.

Also, instead of the commercial food essences and colourings, delicate flavours were obtained by using a fragrant leaf – lemon, orange or bay – or a scrap of lemon or naartjie peel. The secret of success with many puddings including true *melktert* to this day!

Colouring was easily achieved by a pinch of saffron, for yellow, spinach for green, beetroot for purple, and so on. But let's assure you all this including cherished old-timers such as crystallised flowers, flavoured sugars, spiced vinegars and brandied fruits are still easily possible – as proved in these pages, and budget-wise they are winners.

Acknowledging that fresh herbs give a different flavour than do dried herbs still old-time cooks did dry their own, and replenished them in air–tight containers when the season came round again. As for spices, we still wonder at those huge ornamental jars in our museums, once filled with fragrant spices imported from the East. If you feel you are neglecting spices there's no reason why you should not catch up with these traditional ingredients which will cost you little beyond following the advice from Malay and Asiatic chefs in our curry and rystafel sections. Now a word to our younger readers . . .

Straws in the Wind

Many of you young people today are showing an interest in traditional foods. Coupled with a strong tendency to vegetarianism this is a sign of our present age and not to be ignored. At Silwood Kitchen students delight in the baking of wholewheat bread, making preserves and probing the possibilities of the vegetable and herb gardens.

This back-to-nature movement is so encouraging we feel like flaunting it before those other youngsters – millions throughout the world – who have already lost their taste for the real thing and, as a market research programme reveals, actually *prefer* the substitute flavours concocted in a test tube. Unwittingly of course, they are being conditioned admirably for the meal tablets of the future. Yet, personally, we do not think there are many people who would wish to forego the relaxing joys of eating and drinking with their friends, the happy get-together at braai and family table – for a session of chewing pills.

Among the many modern indications showing complete indifference to "good taste" is the common habit of drinking through a straw. When we come to think about it, we are merely slaking our thirst and that could be done traditionally, as the Bushman does, by sucking dew through a reed pushed into the cleft of a plant or shrub. But why not savour to the full our natural fruit juices as we do our wine? No-one drinks wine through a straw. When we drink superb fresh fruit juices or our world-famed Appletiser, for example, it would be an insult to our taste buds to bypass them by using a straw. They are too good to drink through a straw.

To conclude this introductory chapter, our main point is that the past can direct our future towards not only economy and health, but also towards the cultivation of a more sensitive sense of taste. Discrimination learnt by parents is passed on to their children. And we can assure those who study these "survival" recipes (with our adaptations) that there is no need to worry unduly about depressions. Even inflations need not deflate you.

A small garden plot or even a window box can provide vitamins, and in defiance of high fruit or meat prices a girl (maybe you or your daughter) has always the option of befriending a farmer – even if it does mean having to marry him. After that all she needs to remember is *Kissin' don't last. Good cookin do.*

Note: For further information about old South African cookery books consult our *Cookery in Southern Africa Traditional and Today* in your library. Students of cookery can also obtain a bibliography from Silwood Kitchen, Rondebosch, C.P.

Johan van Riebeeck as he stands surveying Adderley Street. After a separation of years, he is now within hailing distance of his wife, Maria de la Quellerie.

A Word from the Publisher

For all of us, richer or poorer, more health conscious or just heartily hungry – this book has the answers from the nostalgic past adapted to present day living.

Our Best Traditional Recipes is not an abridged version of the authors' *Cookery in Southern Africa Traditional and Today,* which at the time of writing (March 1975) is out of print. This smaller book has the additional interest of new ideas and recipes obtained by the authors' further recent research.

Appetizers

Hors-d'oeuvre, cocktail snacks, and those appetising titbits taken before meals cannot be classified as traditional. We refer readers to the relevant chapters in our *Cookery in Southern Africa Traditional and Today* for full details and today's recipes. The few included in these pages will be found under Cocktails in the *Index* at the end of this book.

Probably the nearest our farmer pioneers got to cocktail snacks was when they chewed on a piece of biltong and, as for their labourers, we are reminded of a tribal custom that got the gastric juices flowing adequately in a costless cunning way. Our Black domestic, Anne, explained:

'When we are hungry, when crops fail and we do not like to kill our money (cattle), we grind the mealies and make porridge and on top of each person's porridge is put a little bit of dried meat, like the star on a Christmas tree. The law is that no one is allowed to eat the meat until all the porridge is eaten. So we look at the bit of meat while we eat the porridge until all the porridge is gone. But what happens? So full are we with porridge we don't need the meat'.

Checking this story with Africans from various tribes the fate of the piece of meat varies from 'it just disappears' or 'is given to the dog' or 'saved until next porridge time'.

Salmagundi

Victorian Form of Hors d'Oeuvre

A salmagundi was a sort of vegetable mosaic made with pickled herring, cold dressed chicken, salt beef, radishes, endive, olives, and so on, all arranged with regard to contrast in colour as well as flavour, and served with oil, vinegar, pepper and salt. The following is a good recipe for a Victorian salmagundi:

Take a large round dish; place in the centre a bunch of fresh endive (chicory), and lay round it strips of herring or anchovy interspersed with neat slices from the breast of a chicken. Put round these a band of hardboiled yolk of egg chopped small, then one of green parsley, then slices of red beef or tongue, then the white of the egg, and lastly a garland of sprigs of watercress. Insert trimmed olives, green capers, radishes, barberries, etc., wherever they will be most effective. Serve with salad sauce. Sometimes the herrings for a salmagundi are opened and the flesh is taken out without injuring the skin. It is then minced with an equal quantity of cold chicken and grated ham or tongue, seasoned rather highly, and put back into the skins till they look plump and of good shape.

Sorbets

In the past sorbets were served at banquets between courses to refresh the palate. They consist of half frozen ices of fruit juice sometimes with wine added and a white of egg base. Lemon sorbets have always been popular. Due to lack of space in this short book we give a sorbet suitable for today. (For all other recipes for sherbets and ice creams write to Silwood Kitchen, Rondebosch, C.P.)

Tomato Water-Ice or Sorbet

A Refreshing Starter

For 600 ml (1 pint) of liquid for freezing: 750 g (1¹/₂ lb) good ripe tomatoes, 2 or 3 shallots, finely chopped mint or basil, salt and pepper, freshly ground, to flavour, sugar to taste, lemon juice, ¹/₂ cup water.

Cut up the tomatoes, remove the seeds and cook the flesh to a pulp in ¹/₂ cup water with shallots, herbs and seasoning; rub this through a nylon sieve or aluminium strainer. Add sugar (the amount depends on the ripeness of the tomatoes), add lemon juice to taste (at least the juice of 1 lemon) but bear in mind that it is better to over than under flavour this liquid. The consistency should be thick. Set the freezer box at maximum power and pour the mixture into a well-chilled tray; leave for 20 minutes in the freezer or until stiff. Remove and turn into a bowl. Beat well with a rotary beater. Return mixture to the tray and place in refrigerator box. Freeze for 40–50 minutes. For an even creamier texture the beating process may be repeated after the mixture has been frozen again for 30 minutes. It should then be returned to the freezer for a further 10–20 minutes.

Oyster Cocktails

Place bearded oysters in cocktail glasses and pour the following sauce over: Combine equal quantities of tomato soup (tinned or home-made) and salad cream, adding Worcestershire sauce and a little sugar to taste.

Grape Appetizers

With Cream Cheese

Here is the way to make tempting appetizers of fresh grapes. Use any large table grapes that are available. Stem, wash and dry the grapes, and split each open far enough to remove the seeds. Stuff them with softened cream cheese, blended with salt, freshly-ground pepper, and a pinch of sugar. Let some cheese spill out of the tops. Toast slivered almond until lightly browned. Sprinkle with salt, and dip the stuffed grapes in the nuts. Place on toothpicks and arrange on a tray.

❊   ❊   ❊

The Bantu enjoys dried mealie kernels when he goes on a journey in the same way as peasants in the East prepare their chick peas by parching in a pan and then take with them when they travel.

Note: For further Appetisers refer to *Index* under *Cocktail Snacks.*

Soups

and liquid refreshment

Potage Germiny

This soup was served to M. André Simon, C.B.E., M.M., at the dinner given in his honour by the Gourmet Society at Silwood Kitchen on 12th March, 1965.

250 g (¹/₂ lb) sorrel (without stems), 60 g (2 oz) butter, 3 chicken (or beef) cubes, 6 egg yolks, 1 cup cream.

Take some French sorrel*, wash it well, drain and remove the stems. Keep it in the refrigerator until required. Chop sorrel up a little, then wilt it in the butter, swishing it around with a wooden spoon. Pass it through a fine sieve, and to 1 cup of this pulp add 6 cups of broth, made with the chicken (or beef) cubes. Heat the mixture until it boils. Next place the yolks of the eggs and 1 large cup of cream in a bowl, and beat them together. Add 1 spoon of hot stock to the cold mixture, to prevent curdling, then combine all, and season well with salt, pepper and monosodium glutamate. The addition of a little puréed spinach is an improvement.

Lentil Soup

After cleaning the lentils, boil in water in a saucepan. Brown a slice of ham or bacon with a sliced onion in a fry pan, using a little fat. When this is cooked, add lentils and let all simmer, adding a little white wine or white vinegar. Before serving, stir in the beaten yolk of one egg and season to taste.

Vineyard Soup

Judy Desmond in *Traditional Cookery in Southern Africa* gives the recipe for a soup that could have been made by the Huguenots as it belonged to the old-time vineyard workers of Europe. The buds of leaves from the vines are its basic ingredient. After the large buds have been scaled they are tied in bunches and stewed in a soup pot together with a turnip and a diced carrot and 1 clove of garlic with seasonings. The small buds of the leaves are kept aside. When the soup is ready it is strained and the small buds added and, last of all, small cubes of bread are thrown in.

---

* French sorrel, easily grown and traditional in South Africa, should be sown from seed or cuttings about August. It has a large acid-tasting leaf, not unlike spinach in appearance. There are many culinary uses for this herb. One of the most popular is, cut up finely, as a piquant flavouring for omelettes, soups or salads.

Restorers . . . Restaurants

In Seventeenth Century France, soups were known as 'restorers' and those places where one was restored became known as restaurants. Originally these restaurants specialised in chicken soup.

Brown Chicken Soup

Traditional South African

> Carcase, giblets, feet, neck and any scraps of stuffing (about one table-spoon), 30 g (1 oz) butter, 2 small onions (or 3 shallots), 1 medium-sized tomato, a pinch of basil, celery if available, 30 g (1 oz) flour and browning, seasoning according to the stuffing.

Place all in a saucepan with $1^1/_2$ litres ($2^1/_2$ pints) water, cover and simmer for 2 hours. Strain and cool. Skim off any fat. Add chopped cooked liver and the flesh of the chicken if you want 'pieces' in the soup. Otherwise omit and serve strained. Add browning to the flour with butter and, when blended into a *roux,* add to the strained stock. Serve hot with fried bread croutons.

Cockaleekie

Ancient recipe

Pluck and draw an old cock (an old hen would be too fat for this soup). Without trussing lay him in a bed of barley and sliced leeks in a big saucepan. Season well with pepper and salt, then pour 3 litres of water over and allow all to simmer for hours until the cock is rags and the barley and leeks are pulp. Serve without the bones in a rich mush.

Hello to the Chicken Carcase

We said goodbye long ago to Great-Granny's stockpot always a-simmer at the side of the stove ready for every bone and scrap of savoury food. But today it is 'hello' to the chicken carcase, simmered the day after the flesh has been consumed (no later for safety's sake) and every scrap of stuffing and skin adding to the richness and flavour. That delicate jelly formed when the stock is cold and the value of the rich layer of dripping ready for frying have convinced us all chicken is the best buy when meat is short.

Yet we can occasionally get bones from the butcher, and because stock for soups, sauces and casseroles is a valuable traditional asset in the kitchen here is how to make stock the traditional chef's way.

Light Bone Stock

> 1 kg (2 lb) beef bones (sawn or chopped), 2 coarsely sliced carrots, 2 coarsely sliced onions, 1 leek (the white part only), small stalk of celery - when available, 6 peppercorns, a bouquet garni, salt, 2 .5 litres (4 pints) cold water.

Wash the bones carefully and put them with the vegetables, herbs and seasoning into a large pan. Add the water and bring the stock to the boil quite quickly, without a lid. Skim the surface carefully. Cover the stock with the lid and simmer the stock uninterruptedly for 3 to 4 hours. (Turning the heat on and off is apt to turn it sour.) Strain the liquid off the bones and leave it over-night. Next day skim the fat from the surface, but keep it and clarify it for frying and making casseroles (see further on).

Brown Stock

Some soups and casseroles require a brown stock. For this use bones and vegetables as given in the recipe for light stock. Dry them carefully, which helps them to brown more quickly, and put them into a roasting tin in a hot oven. When the tops of the bones and vegetables are brown, turn them over and give the others a chance to colour. Afterwards put them into the large pan and continue making the stock in the same way as the white stock.

Many different ingredients can be used for stock. Veal bones are good, so are chicken or turkey carcasses with bacon rinds added for extra flavour. Simply simmer the bones or carcasses with the vegetables and strain them afterwards. Bacon bones are also good, but should be used with caution as they tend to be rather salty.

To Clarify Fat or Dripping

Put the fat into a pan and cover it with cold water; bring it to the boil and pour it into a basin. Leave to get quite cold, overnight if possible. Next day, lift off the cake of fat which has formed on top of the liquid, and scrape away any liquid which sticks to it. Put the fat into a strong pan and boil it up until it stops bubbling, by which time all the water will have evaporated and pure fat will remain. Strain it into a basin through a fine strainer or a piece of muslin.

❉   ❉   ❉

An advertisement that appeared in Cape Town, 1822 (according to Laidler's *Tavern of the Ocean),* ran as follows:

Lovers Of Good Eating

TURTLE SOUP

At the London Hotel, Hout Street

A fine fresh Turtle, just arrived from the Island of Ascension will be dressed this morning by a professional cook (late turtle dresser to His Excellency the late Acting Governor) and sold at the following prices: per pint 3 rds, per quart 5 rds, per gallon 20 rds.

The late acting governor we presume was Sir Rufane Donkin and thereby hangs a tale told in our *Cookery in Southern Africa Traditional and Today,* with more about turtles. Here as a sop to the past we give in explicit detail an old mock turtle soup recipe for those who do not wish to use a packeted soup.

Mock Turtle Soup
Old Recipe

Half a calf's head (your butcher can get it for you), 125 g ($^1/_4$ lb) butter, same quantity of lean ham, 2 tablespoons minced parsley, a little minced thyme, a little sweet marjoram and basil, 2 onions, a few chopped mushrooms, 2 shallots, 2 tablespoons of flour, $1^1/_2$ dozen forcemeat balls about the size of a nutmeg, cayenne and salt to suit your taste, the juice of 1 lemon, a Seville orange, 1 dessertspoon of pounded sugar, and $3^3/_4$ litres (3 quarts) of stock.

Take the half a calf's head with the skin on, remove the brains, and lay them aside; wash the head in several waters, and let it soak in cold water for an hour. Put it into a stewpan, cover with cold water, let it boil gently for an hour, and carefully remove the scum as it rises. Cut the meat from the bones, and divide it with the tongue into small neat squares of about 2 .5 cm (1''). Let these cool, put them into a saucepan, cover with the stock, and let them boil gently until they are tender without being overdone. Melt 125 g (4 oz) of butter in a saucepan, and put in 90 g (3 oz) lean, undressed ham cut into dice; a sliced carrot, 2 tablespoons of chopped parsley, a tablespoon of mixed sweet herbs, of which 2/5ths shall be sweet marjoram, 2/5ths basil, and 1/5th thyme, 2 chopped onions, and 1 or 2 chopped mushrooms when they are to be had. Stir these over the fire for 2 or 3 minutes, then pour over them 600 ml (1 pint) of stock, and let them simmer gently for 2 hours. Moisten 2 tablespoons of flour with a little cold stock, and add this to the seasoning stock. Let it boil; add the remainder of the stock, and rub the soup through a fine hair sieve. Put it back into the saucepan with the pieces of meat, boil all gently together for a few minutes, add a glassful of wine, a tablespoon of lemon juice, and salt and pepper if required.

Have the forcemeat balls ready prepared, put them into the tureen, pour the soup over them, and serve very hot. Sufficient for 12.

Welsh Leek Broth

1 gammon knuckle of ham, or a thick piece af salt bacon, 500 g (1 lb) potatoes (peeled), 6 carrots (cut into small pieces), 1 large bunch of leeks (thinly sliced), 1 cabbage (finely shredded), 25 ml (2 tablespoons) oatmeal, a little cold water, seasoning to taste, chopped parsley for garnishing.

Cook gammon knuckle with peeled potatoes and carrots on a low heat for about 1¹/₂ hours. Remove gammon knuckle and add thinly sliced leeks and finely shredded cabbage. Thicken the soup by mixing the oatmeal to a stiff paste with a little cold water and adding gradually to the mixture. Stir well and when the vegetables are soft season to taste, Add chopped parsley and serve.

Our Pumpkin Soup

2 tablespoons butter, 1 onion (chopped), 750 g (1¹/₂ lb) pumpkin (peeled and diced), 4 cups chicken stock – or cubes may be used, ¹/₂ teaspoon salt, 2 tablespoons flour, 1 tablespoon butter, salt, pepper and Aromat, ³/₄ cup fresh cream, 1 tablespoon butter (a little cinnamon if liked).
Garnish: toasted croutons, lightly salted whipped fresh cream.

Melt the butter in a large saucepan, add chopped onion and cook gently until onions are almost soft but not brown. Add pumpkin, chicken stock, and salt. Simmer the pumpkin until it is soft. Stir in the flour kneaded with one tablespoon butter and bring the soup to the boil. Rub the soup through a fine sieve or purée it in a blender. Check the seasoning and add cream and one tablespoon of butter. Heat the soup just to the boiling point and serve it garnished with tiny toasted croûtons and lightly salted whipped cream. Yield: 6–8 portions.

Lady Anne Barnard

The Castle, the *Kasteel de Goede Hoop,* South Africa's oldest building replaced Jan van Riebeeck's small earthern fort in 1679. As a social centre it lapsed from importance when the British seized the Cape in 1795 and the Governor decided not to live there. But Lady Anne Barnard the vivacious wife of the Governor's Secretary revived the glories of the Castle's past with her elegant parties. When we visit the beautifully kept restored Castle today we feel again her presence and realise her enrichment of the entertaining side of our social history.

Lady Anne's Vegetable Soup

While staying at Paradise Cottage* during 1798 Lady Anne Barnard writes in her Journal: 'Two Black cooks from town are come to assist me, as a dozen of people are to dine here, whom my husband has invited, finding them anxious to see this little place. I have late succeeded so well in a vegetable soup that I can make no greater present to the persons reading this (if they reside in the country) than by giving them the following':

Take one large head of celery and shred it down, stopping before you reach the green part which is bitter; take one onion, a handful of spinach, three heads of cabbage, each about the size of your two hands, half a dozen leaves of sorrel, twenty carrots twice as long as your finger, two or three handfuls of green peas; and after you have shelled them, if the peas are young (but not otherwise) you may cut the shells in pieces and throw them in with the rest. All these must be cut into bits about the size of your little finger, and the carrots smaller than sixpences. Put all in a large wash-hand basin, which will be sufficient to make a small tureen full.

Meantime take a quarter of a pound of butter, put it into a frying pan and when melted dust in a handful of flour. Stir it well about in the pan till it is of the colour of brown tanned leather. Then put your vegetables and that into a saucepan, with as much gravy or weak broth as will cover them all over, and stand two inches above them. Let it stew gently for two or three hours till all is quite tender. Put a large teaspoon of salt to it and another of pepper. Then having given it five minutes more, serve it up hot in your tureen. If the liquid is taken from it, it will be equally good as stewed vegetables.

And Lady Anne concluded happily, *Our friends arrived and did it ample justice.*

Lady Anne's browning of flour and butter into a *roux* is the secret of success with many soups as is the frying of vegetables in butter before making the soup, usual with our favourite traditional soups.

---

* The ruins of Paradise Cottage can still be seen in the woods near Paradise Road, Newlands, C.P. When Lady Anne found the cottage too small another summer residence was built, namely The Vineyard – today one of the Cape's most elegant hotels.

Limpet or Periwinkle Soup

Mrs Cloete of Alphen

The Cloete name at the Cape goes back to Jan van Riebeeck's time and it is interesting to know that *Hildagonda's* recipe came from a Mrs Cloete at Alphen. Today Mr Bairnsfather Cloete owns that dignified Cape Alphen House in the Alphen estate. To dine in this old Cape home is a pleasure indulged in by those who know good food, and much of it is traditional.

For the limpet soup you are advised to collect half a bucketful from the rocks below low tide mark in the winter months, their season. Put them in fresh water to kill them and rid of sand. Scrape the shells clean, pound them in a mortar, put in a pot, cover with water and boil. When done, strain through a coarse linen cloth, and add good beef or mutton stock in the proportion of 1 cup to every 3 cups of periwinkle broth. A couple of onions should be boiled in the meat stock. One dozen peppercorns, the same of allspice, one tablespoon of flour, and one of burnt sugar are added to the mixed stocks. Lastly, it is poured into a tureen into which a good tumbler of wine has been put, and served with sippets of toast.

Onion Soup au Gratin

3 large onions (thinly sliced), 25 ml (2 tablespoons butter), 12 .5 ml (1 tablespoon) flour, 6 x 250 ml (6 cups) bouillon, salt and pepper, sprinkling of Aromat (MSG), pinch of sugar, slices crisp French bread, 125 g ($^1/_4$ lb) Gruyère cheese, grated – or strong Cheddar cheese.

Cook the onion in the butter until golden-brown. Sprinkle it with flour and brown lightly. Add the bouillon and seasonings, and simmer for 10 minutes. Cover the soup with bread slices. Ladle a little soup over the bread and let it stand for about 5 minutes. Sprinkle the surface with cheese and put the dish under the broiler for a minute or two, just enough to melt the cheese. If there is not enough room to put it under the broiler, you can serve the soup in individual earthenware dishes, after putting these under the grill.

Traditional Bean Soup

250 g ($^1/_2$ lb) haricot beans, 2 large onions, 5 tablespoons oil, 4 rashers of bacon (squares of cheese toast for vegetarians), 1 tablespoon self-raising flour, salt, pepper, garlic powder.

Fry the onions and bacon in the oil until golden brown and add the washed haricot beans. Sprinkle them with the flour; when the beans are well coated, add enough water or stock to cover them. Season, and add the garlic powder. Cover the pot and let it simmer until the beans are very soft and mashy. Strain them through a sieve, and boil again. Serve plain, or with fried croûtons.

Variations: Dress up bean soup for good taste by adding: some small herb dumplings; squares of Welsh rarebit; any sausages sliced in circles; pieces of crisp fried bacon.

Today's Gazpacho

Add to a carton of thick yoghurt a little of the following, all coarsely chopped: raw tomatoes (skinned), celery, chives, cucumber, almonds, and $^1/_2$ clove garlic (crushed), a little salt and sugar to taste. Mix all together to attain a thinnish soup of a pouring consistency. Serve ice cold.

To Flavour Milk for Stock or Soup

Put the milk in a saucepan and add 4–6 peppercorns, a blade of mace, parsley stalks, a slice of onion, a slice of carrot and a bay leaf. Heat slowly to scalding point and strain.

For All Cream Soups

The consistency of cream soup should be that of day-old cream. Take equal quantities of béchamel sauce and prepared vegetables. Tomatoes, peas, asparagus, mushrooms, potatoes, cauliflower, carrots or spinach. For the luxury touch, just before serving add a topping of whipped cream.

The Basic Béchamel Sauce

30 g (1 oz) butter, 1 tablespoon flour, 1 cup warmed milk (or stock), 1 tablespoon cream, salt and pepper to taste.

Melt the butter in a saucepan, add the flour and stir over a low heat, using a wooden spoon. This is called a roux and should be well cooked. Remove saucepan from the heat and, very gradually, add the liquid (milk or stock), stirring all the time, return to the heat and cook and thicken. Carefully add the cream and season to taste.

To Whip Evaporated Milk

Evaporated milk can be whipped into a good foam by chilling the milk in a bowl until fine ice crystals form in the milk around the edge of the bowl. When the milk is whipped, add two teaspoons of lemon juice or vinegar for each cup of milk.

CHILLED MILK DRINKS

Macaroon Milk

Flavour milk with almond extract. Pour into a glass and sprinkle the top with sifted, crushed mcaroons (about 2 macaroons to 1 glass of milk). Serve cold.

Milk Ginger

$^3/_4$ cup milk, $^1/_4$ cup ginger ale, sugar if desired.

Mix milk and ginger ale, sweeten to taste and serve cold.

Spiced Milk

$^3/_4$ cup milk, spice (cinnamon, cloves or nutmeg).

Mix spice with the milk, sweeten to taste and, if desired, add a small stream of soda water.

Caramel Milk

1 cup milk, 1 tablespoon sugar, speck of salt.

Put the sugar in a smooth saucepan and stir until the syrup is a brown colour. Add 2 tablespoons water and let simmer until it becomes the consistency of thick syrup, let cool, then stir into the milk. Serve cold.

HOT MILK DRINKS

Cinnamon and Orange Flip

1 stick cinnamon, 2 tablespoons sugar, 600 ml (1 pint) milk, orange rind.

Infuse the cinnamon and orange rind in milk till the milk is well flavoured, then remove them. Add sugar and heat till nearly boiling. Pour into glasses and serve.

Jamaican Punch

2 bananas, 1 tablespoon castor sugar, 1 tablespoon rum, 300 ml ($^1/_2$ pint) milk.

Mash bananas and mix with sugar and rum. Pour into glasses and fill with hot milk. Serve straight away.

Egg Nog

2 eggs, 3 teaspoons sugar, 600 ml (1 pint) milk.

Break the eggs and beat together with the sugar. Heat the milk and, when almost boiling, pour onto eggs, etc., stirring all the time.

Hot Butterscotch

12 butterscotch sweets, 600 ml (1 pint) milk.

Melt the butterscotch carefully over a low heat, then add milk, bring to the boil and serve. A little cream may be added if desired.

Savoury Shake

3 eggs, 600 ml (1 pint) milk, 3 dessertspoons tomato ketchup, 3 teaspoons Yorkshire relish or Worcestershire sauce, pinch of salt and cayenne pepper.

Heat the milk, then beat in the other ingredients.

❉   ❉   ❉

Buttermilk

Buttermilk, is, of course, the acidulous liquid remaining after the butter has been churned out. Although the modern taste is returning to buttermilk, in the past it was a popular health drink – almost a beauty potion. But they didn't know in those old days just how few calories it had compared with full milk (200 calories to buttermilk's 120). So now the dairies are making it available there is a growing demand for buttermilk, alongside the ever-more-popular yoghurt – indicative of the swing back to the dairy products of our forefathers who, although they had never heard of a vitamin and shunned slimming, knew more than a thing or two about good food and drink.

There are more ways than drinking buttermilk plain. Ring the changes by: combining with fruit juices, adding jam or apple purée, for example, or even by combining it with tomato juice. And to bring out the best of the flavour and smoothness, do try beating well with an egg whisk – which homogenises it (distributes the fat particles).

Chilled Buttermilk

Place the contents of 600 ml (1 pint) of chilled buttermilk in a bowl and whisk until frothing. Serve either plain or topped with a little cinnamon sugar, or honey. Pineapple, guavas, apricot and apple juices (sweetened) can be combined.

Buttermilk Egg Nog

1 cup buttermilk, 1 egg, salt and sugar if desired.

Beat the egg thoroughly. Add salt or sugar and buttermilk and beat until light and foamy.

Yoghurt

Once made at home – still possible if you obtain a plant from a health store – yoghurt, like other fermented milks, has a fine curd easier on the digestion than whole milk. Both the thick variety known as Bulgarian, which combines well with fruit, and the thin drinking yoghurt are obtainable from dairies.

Apple Yoghurt
Serve it for Breakfast

2 eating apples, juice of $\frac{1}{2}$ lemon, 1 large carton yoghurt (the thick type), a little honey. (Serves 2.)

Core and slice the apples thinly into a bowl. Sprinkle with lemon juice. Mix $\frac{3}{4}$ of the apple slices into the yoghurt, reserving remainder for decoration. Divide into 2 individual dishes, pour a little honey over and decorate with apple slices.

Calabash Milk

Among the kitchen utensils in our museums there is always a variety of gourds, the hollow calabash shells which were used as containers for all kinds of things, some fitted with lids. Some of these gourds were for the making of calabash milk or sour milk. Sour milk (*masi* or *maas*) was considered to be better for growing children than fresh milk, by Boer farmer and Bantu alike.

Calabash milk, according to experts, should never be distinguished by a raw flavour. An old farming authority advises that if the calabash after some use continues to impart a 'raw calabashy flavour' to the milk, a remedy is to fill the calabash with buttermilk a few times and the calabash flavour will disappear. The authority explains that to make good calabash milk, 'use whole milk, and do not let it get too sour or too old in the calabash. Always leave a little of the old milk in the calabash, never quite empty it, or you will not have it ready for use daily. The little old milk which you leave will turn the fresh milk, and so turn it into calabash milk without too long a delay. Fill with fresh whole milk every evening. You will soon learn to make it exactly to the taste of your family.' Some like it with a real 'sour tang'.

Oatmeal Water

A substitute for milk evolved by trekking farmers of the old days was made by pouring 2 cups of boiling water on a tablespoon of coarse oatmeal and stirring. When cool it was strained through cloth and added to tea or coffee.

Milking

Watch out – Cows are Fussy

'Slow milkers gradually dry up a cow, the faster and more gentle a cow is milked the better' advises that old *South African Household Guide* – which goes on to say that in some cases cows refuse to be milked by Whites if they have been used to Black milkers. We wonder if they are more contented with today's mechanical milking machines?

Dairy milk in urban areas today is pasteurised. This means that before bottling it is heated then quickly cooled and bottled. Thus the milk souring organisms are reduced. Farm milk, unpasteurised, is usually available in country districts.

For Milk Drinks: When making milk drinks whole milk powder, skim milk powder condensed or evaporated milk may also be used. Follow the instructions on the container.

❖   ❖   ❖

Fresh Citrus Drinks

Oranges and lemons should be squeezed immediately before drinking to preserve the vitamin content to the full. Serve fresh with natural brown sugar and water and ice cubes to taste.

Real fruit syrups like Granny made are as easily made today. For Silwood Kitchen's demonstration method of bottling syrups refer to our *Cookery in Southern Africa Traditional and Today* in your library or write to Silwood Kitchen for a leaflet. (Address Silwood Road, Rondebosch, C.P.)

Lemon Syrup

To 10 cups of lemon juice add 8 cups of sugar. Put on to boil, and from the time it comes to the boil keep it on for 20 minutes, but not longer, or the colour will be spoiled. Do not use an aluminium pan, as this will darken the syrup. Bottle when hot, but allow to cool before corking. This is a delicious recipe and will keep indefinitely if well corked. If granadillas are available, substitute 2 cups of granadilla pulp for 2 of the lemon juice. This gives the syrup a delightful and unusual flavour.

Lemon Imperial

Wash 4 large lemons, cut them in half and squeeze out the juice. Cut up the skins, removing pith and pips. Put the lemon juice, skins and $3/4$ cup sugar in a jug. Pour on 1.25 litres (2 pints) fresh boiling water. Cover and allow to stand overnight. Remove the skins, strain and serve as cold as possible with ice and diluted to taste with water.

Camomile Tea

Taken cold, camomile tea was said to be beneficial in cases of hysteria, headache or dyspepsia. It was also used as a mild emetic when that was required. It was made by soaking 5 drachms of camomile flowers in 600 ml (pint) of hot water; pouring the boiling water over the flowers to infuse for 10 minutes, then straining.

Barley Water

This health-giving drink is seldom made at home now but it has a deserved reputation for cleansing the system and is very palatable when sweetened and with fresh lemon juice added. Put a handful of washed pearl barley in a large saucepan with a pinch of salt and pour boiling water on it; let it simmer until the barley is tender then strain and cool; diluting it with more boiled water and lemon juice until it reaches the desired thinness. Sugar to taste.

Some old recipes advise clearing the barley from cloudiness by boiling the washed barley for 10 minutes then draining and boiling up with water as indicated above.

Rose Hip Syrup

An Old Reviver Revived

Rose-hips give a syrup which is very rich in vitamin C. To retain this vitamin choose hips which are fresh, fully ripe and deep red. Crush, grate or mince them and put at once into boiling water, allowing 1.9 litres (3 pints) per 1 kg (2 lb) hips. Bring back to boiling point, then remove from the heat and allow to stand for 10–15 minutes. Strain through a scalded cloth or jelly-bag and when it ceases to drip, return the pulp to the pan with another 900 ml ($1\frac{1}{2}$ pints) boiling water. Re-boil and let stand as before for 10 minutes, then strain. Mix the two extracts; pour into a clean pan and reduce by boiling until the juice measures 900 ml ($1\frac{1}{2}$ pints). Add 500 g (1 lb) sugar. Stir until dissolved and boil for 5 minutes. Pour while hot into clean, hot sterilised bottles and seal at once.

Papaw Syrup

A South African Summer Drink

The following is a delicious summer drink, and has been suggested specially for those suffering from indigestion.

Cover the seeds of 2 large papaws with boiling water. Allow to stand for 2 or 3 hours. Strain, add lemon and sugar to taste and cold water to make a liquid equal to 1.2 litres (2 pints).

A Soothing Syrup

Lady Anne Barnard's Recipe

After the return of her husband to England, Lady Anne and Andrew settled down at Gothic House, Wimbledon. The year was 1805 and at 55 years of age Anne was still contemplating life with a youthful eye. During this period Andrew fell ill with influenza and she remembered the remedy her mother used when she was ill as a child. She immediately set about preparing it and fondly nursing him back to health. The medicine was meant to soothe the patient's chest. It was prepared from the decoction of linseed and of liquorice stick, bruised and boiled over a low fire in a pint of water, and then strained and mixed with powdered sugar-candy, lemon juice and rum. The nostrum cured Andrew, and though his health was not all Anne could have wished, 'he seemed in excellent spirits.'

Brews and Potions

Caudles, possets, syllabubs and tansies. Space does not permit us to give the recipes for these stimulating concoctions enjoyed by weary travellers arriving at an inn by coach or horseback. They all had some ingredients in common – alcohol, eggs, milk or cream, or gruel for thickening. They served the good purpose of reviving with more safety than hard liquor while the traveller waited for mine host to cook a meal. An example is the simplest syllabub we have come across, made by milking a cow direct into a bucket containing white wine – with a frothy result.

And for that cold shiver at dawn? In mid-18th century Cape Town it was customary for the gentry to take a *sopie* (small glass of gin or brandy) before breakfast. And instead of our cocktails visitors starting a meal would often be offered a glass of wine with aloe or wormwood as bitters.

Orange Brandy

3 bottles brandy (Oude Meester), very thinly pared peel of 12 large Seville oranges, very thinly pared peel of 6 lemons, 1.5 kg (3 lb) castor sugar.

Steep the peel in brandy for 3 weeks. Strain and add the sugar to the brandy, and shake well. Shake well together every day until the sugar has dissolved. There is no need to boil the sugar. When the sugar has dissolved, clarify and bottle. Cork well. Keep the demijohn well corked throughout the process.

Cold Constantia Punch

1 bottle red wine (claret type), 1 glass Van der Hum, 10 tablespoons sugar, 6 cloves, 1 sliced orange, liqueur brandy.

Pour the wine into a saucepan and add the sliced orange, sugar and cloves. Bring nearly to the boil. Boil 600 ml (1 pint) of water and add this to the mixture. Add 1 glass of Van der Hum and 1 glass of brandy. Stir. Pour into glasses and grate a little nutmeg on top of each.

English Mulled Wines

1820 Settler's Recipe

Boil some spice in a little water till the flavour is gained, then add an equal quantity of port, some sugar and nutmeg; heat and serve with toast. Another way is to boil a bit of cinnamon and some grated nutmeg a few minutes in a large teacup of water, then pour into it a pint of port wine, and add sugar to taste; heat it up and it will be ready to drink.

Egg Flip

Old English Recipe Using Ale

Beat 2 or 3 eggs with 90 g (3 oz) sugar, and throw this into a jug of pale ale that has been made warm but not heated too much. Now throw both back into an empty jug. Repeat 6 times until all is well mixed. Serve in glasses while hot with a grating of ginger and nutmeg over the top.

Coffee

The first quarter of the 19th century in Cape Town was a period of hotel development and English style taverns appeared. The proprietor of Randalls Coffee Rooms at 1 Grave Street announced that clients would be supplied with genuine coffee at early morning gunfire with gravy and pea soup at 11 a.m. Table beer and fine pale ale was also served . . .

The words genuine coffee are significant. Since the failure of the Duth East India Company's crops, coffee had to be imported and many were the ways of extending it or making substitutes. Oldsters in the Clanwilliam district told us how in times of shortages and war coffee was made from stale bread toasted with sugar, ground acorns, carrots, ripe figs, roots of the *witgatboom* and wild almond tree (for *ghookoffie*) not to mention the common practice of browning mealie meal.

Coffee and tea being imported luxuries* we are not surprised to read of the many substitutes for coffee or of the popularity of *vlei* and bush teas. Our full story about bush tea is contained in *Cookery in Southern Africa Traditional and Today*. It is a success story because the therapeutic value of bush tea is now acknowledged and much is exported.

As for South Africans today, many like to mix bush tea with ordinary tea, anything up to half of each; while thousands drink it made as their forefathers did.

Traditional Method for Making Bush Tea

Use about 1 cup of bush tea (washed in hot water) to 6 cups boiling water and let it stand on the stove and simmer for an hour. This tea can stand on the stove all day ('because this does no harm') to be served with hot milk, half and half, when required. For modern methods of making follow instructions on the packets of the various commercial brands found at supermarkets.

Iced Rooitea

One of Many Recipes

Take 2 level teaspoons Rooitea per cup of boiling water. (It is unnecessary to wash the packet teas.) Pour boiling water on Rooitea and steep for a few minutes. It becomes stronger if boiled a short time. Pour through a fine strainer and cool. Dilute with iced water. Add ice cubes, fresh lemon juice and sugar to taste. Serve chilled with sprigs of mint or lemon circlets.

✳   ✳   ✳

Our First Lady Entertains

Nothing is recorded of Maria entertaining for almost a year after the Van Riebeecks arrival at Table Bay in April 1652. The leaky temporary shed with sail covering was inadequate to cope with the Cape's winter rains and no wonder many of the household became sick, Maria included. But in August she moved into her new house at the (first) Fort and had Hottentot Herry to dine. So much depended on an understanding with the indigenous peoples!

---

* Today thanks to the expertise of our Kenya refugees coffee is being increasingly grown successfully in South Africa.

Sea-foods

Fish and Shellfish

Most well-known of all the street cries of old Cape Town and our youth was the fish horn, a trumpet made of a conically rolled sheet from a paraffin tin and fitted with a mouth piece. These ear shatterers were passed down from fish hawker to hawker's son through the generations. They superseded the street cry produced by blowing through a tube of dried kelp (sea bamboo) as seen in old prints, hanging from the necks of hawkers about the middle of the 19th century. What a far cry it is from those days when fish could be bought for anything from a penny up to a shilling apiece, according to kind and size!

Because fish begins to deteriorate immediately it is removed from its habitat, the water, there is no better way than cooking it fresh from the sea or stream on to the coals.

Fisherman's Method

Any old-timer who likes to catch his fish and eat it on the spot swears by the following way of cooking. This method works best with freshwater fish and the more delicate varieties. He wraps it, scales and all, in wet newspapers and leaves it in the hot coals of the campfire until the outer layers of the paper have burned brown. When the fish is unwrapped it will be found that the scales and skin will come away with the paper.

Another method, beloved of the angler-camper who wants fish for early morning breakfast, is to clean the fish at night, remove the heads, season the inside and wrap each fish in well-greased white paper, then into several sheets of wet newspaper. A trench is then dug deep enough to allow an inch of earth on top and the fish put into the trench. A good camp fire is built on top and the camper presumably enjoys the fire and goes to sleep to awake and unearth his fish beautifully cooked for breakfast.

Cooking Your Catch with Wine

For Gourmet Fishermen

For you who enjoy nothing in this world more than cooking your own 'catch' over an open fire, here are two sophisticated recipes, using white wine.

Tunny: Slice fish about 25 mm (1″) thick and marinate for 3–4 hours in white wine. Then season fish with salt, pepper and Aromat. Place fish slices in an oiled tin directly on the braai coals and cook until tender.

Cape Harders and Galjoen: Scrape and clean fish, leaving the skin, head and tail. Marinate for an hour or two in white wine. Split the fish, insert parsley, seasoning and a knob of butter. Wrap individually in foil and place right in amongst the embers. Bake for 15 minutes or until cooked. Serve with a chilled white wine.

Our Fish in Van der Stel's Day

One of the earliest paintings of Cape fish is that of the freshwater yellow fish of the Western Cape by the artist Claudius who went with Simon van der Stel on his Namaqualand journey in 1685. About 1687, Simon van der Stel made a special trip to False Bay and the party caught many 'unknown' fishes from boats. Claudius's paintings of some of these and other fishes found in Table Bay have recently been discovered and are now in the Africana Museum in Johannesburg. Fish shown are the roman, electric ray, joseph, sunfish, gurnurd, yellowtail, oarfish, bulleye and horsefish.

The quick commercial freezing of fish today means we need not salt, smoke or wind dry it as our forefathers did. Yet, almost paradoxically, a taste for smoked meats and fish has returned to favour – for flavour. Fishermen we know enjoy smoking their catch in one of those compact modern smokers obtainable from sports specialist shops. It is said that the flavour of the smoking depends on the special sawdust used – usually from Sweden. Why import it? Silwood Kitchen hopes for an answer one day!

General Rules for Cooking Fish

Lean fish include: haddock, stockfish, kingklip, sole, silver fish and shell fish.

Oily fish are: mackerel, trout, pilchard, salmon, galjoen, Cape salmon and yellowtail (albacore).

Generally speaking, cook oily fish with no extra fat, merely a brushing of oil or butter and dress with lemon juice instead of a creamy rich sauce. Contrarily, dry-fleshed fish may be cooked with fat and accompanied by a rich sauce. Oily fish and fresh water fish are liable to deteriorate rapidly as the fat is distributed throughout the body, whereas white fish have the fat concentrated in the liver. Shellfish decompose rapidly.

Certain survivors from the smokey past are popular today. Examples include haddock and kippers, and in the Cape, of course, snoek.

Snoek

Our Delicatessen Fish

Smoked snoek, always a favourite for flaking on toast, for sandwiches and as an hors d'oeuvre is considered one of our Cape delicatessen foods; while salted, wind-dried snoek is seen today hanging from the rafters of small shops and markets as our great-grannies knew it and is the standby of those who cannot afford refrigerators for all their traditional smoorvis, kedgerees, fish stews and pies. In the Malmesbury district snoek biltong is still made from lightly pickled wind-dried snoek – and considered a speciality of the Swartland.

Old Kaapenaars tell us how they enjoyed Ouma's home-made brown bread spread with lard or sheeptail fat topped with cooked snoek and moskonfyt – a sweet-sour treat certainly Eastern in origin that you can try today. (Refer to Moskonfyt in *Index*.)

Cooking Snoek

As fresh snoek tends to go bad quickly the entrails must be removed soon after it is caught. It is best fried cut in suitable pieces, well coated with egg and breadcrumbs after being dipped in slightly salted flour. It may also be baked. If steamed the fish can be served cold with a vinaigrette dressing and salads. Some people find mayonnaise rather rich with snoek.

Smoorvis or Gesmoorde Vis

Braised Fish

Smoorvis or gesmoorde vis, the traditional Voortrekker recipe, probably came from the East with the Malays. It is interesting to note that similar recipes are found in the West Indies, Mauritius and Madagascar to this day.

> 1 .5 kg (3 lb) dried snoek, soaked overnight (or longer) in water, 2 large onions, sliced, 3 chillies, 6 medium-sized potatoes, cooked rice, chopped parsley.

Drain the fish, remove the bones and shred the flesh. Fry the onions in hot oil and a little butter, until golden-brown. Pound the chillies, and add to the fried onions, together with the diced potatoes. When the potatoes are lightly browned, add the snoek, and braise the mixture until it is lightly browned.

Serve on a bed of cooked rice, with an assortment of side dishes.

South African Pickled Fish

As Made at Silwood Kitchen

> 1¹/₂ kg (3 lb) fresh firm fish (kingklip, kabeljou) or frozen fish (fillets of hake), 3 large onions, 2 cups grape vinegar, 2 cups water, 3 tablespoons sugar, 2 tablespoons mild curry powder, 2 tablespoons Maizena (corn-flour), ¹/₂ teaspoon salt, ¹/₄ teaspoon pepper, Knorr Aromat, a few bay leaves and peppercorns.

Wipe fish with a damp cloth, sprinkle lemon juice over it and season well. Fry the fish in hot oil in the usual way, using no flour or coating, and then remove the skin and bones. Drain on absorbent paper. Mix the Maizena and curry powder together, adding a little of the water, to make a smooth paste. Then add this paste to the remainder of the water, vinegar, onions (which have been sliced in rings), sugar, salt, pepper, Knorr Aromat, bay leaves and peppercorns. Cook until it thickens and the onions are soft.

Pour this sauce over the fish, cool and store in the refrigerator. Serve cold with a green salad.

Pickled Fish Without Curry

Old Recipe

Choose firm-textured fish (either fresh water or sea fish) and cut into 25 mm (1″) thick slices. Sprinkle with salt and pepper and put aside overnight in a cool place, then put the fish in the air until the slices become a little dry. When dry, fry in boiling fat until cooked through. Slice some good onions but not too thinly. Cut up chillies, bay leaves, and add a little turmeric and then simmer all well with the onion in sweetened wine vinegar until the onions are only lightly cooked, stirring the mixture with a wooden spoon. Put the fish into deep earthenware jars (or large-mouthed glass fruit bottles) and layer with onions, repeating until the jars are almost full. Now pour over the vinegar liquid to the brim and cover closely, using the rubber rings and glass tops if you have chosen to use preserving jars. The fish will be ready to serve in 2 or 3 days and if properly bottled should keep for some weeks. (Today we prefer to store in the refrigerator of course.)

Old Variations: Sometimes a little chutney was added to the curry sauce while it simmered or, a bay leaf, ginger and so on. But it should be remembered that vegetable matter combined with the fish does not assist the keeping qualities of the pickle.

Kedgeree

As Hildagonda Approves

This Indian way of dressing cold boiled fish is recommended by our traditional authority, *Hildagonda Duckitt,* for *breakfast.* Now that eggs and bacon are getting beyond the reach of middle income households here is an idea perhaps for today.

250 g (¹/₂ lb) boiled fish, 125 g (¹/₄ lb) rice, 2 eggs, 60 g (2 oz) butter, a little cayenne pepper, salt and nutmeg.

Wash and boil the rice. Break the cooked fish in pieces, taking out all the bones. Put the butter, fish and rice into a stewing pan with cayenne, salt and a grating of nutmeg (not much). Stir well, then add eggs well beaten. Stir over the heat until quite hot. Serve in a hot dish.

Warning from Lesley: Don't let egg mixture attain boiling point. In those 'good' old days such warnings were unnecessary; most girls learnt the principles of cooking at Mother's knee.

Special Kedgeree

Raymond van Niekerk's Recipe

1 packet smoked haddock fillets, 125 ml (¹/₂ cup) milk, 1 tablespoon butter, 2 medium onions, chopped, ¹/₂ cup cream, a pinch of salt and pepper, Aromat, 2 hard-cooked eggs (chopped), grated rind of ¹/₂ lemon, 250 ml (1 cup) cooked rice.

Garnish: Sieved egg yolk, 5 ml (1 teaspoon) chopped parsley. Cook the haddock with the milk in a small saucepan over a moderate heat. Strain off the milk and leave until cold. Melt the butter in a frying pan. Add the chopped onions and sauté until transparent. Stir in the flour to make a *roux.* Gradually add the liquid that the haddock was cooked in, and cook until thick. Just before serving add the warmed cream. Taste to check whether seasoning is correct. Then add the flaked fish, hard-cooked egg whites, lemon rind and rice, and mix well. Garnish with sieved egg yolk and parsley. Serve on toast, or croûtons; or – best of all – on toasted, buttered (British-style) crumpets.

Pickled Herrings

Traditionally 'rollmops'. First soak 6 herrings overnight. Bone and roll them into mops. Boil $1^1/_2$ cups vinegar with bay leaves, allspice and a little sugar. (Use an enamel saucepan.) Allow to cool. Pack alternate layers of onions and herrings into a jar. Pour sauce over and stand for a few days. A richer version may be made by adding 600 ml (1 pint) of cream to the sauce.

De-salting Fish

The unpleasant pungency of salted and smoked fish is easily overcome by covering with water, vinegar and water, or wine and water, and pouring off and replenishing the water from time to time when cooking. Examples are smoked haddock and salted herrings. The cooking of the haddock in milk and water and the herrings in wine further expunges the smoky, salty pungency of the food. Dress kippers and haddock with lemon juice and a knob of butter.

Fish Pie

When you see the pilchards and maasbankers *(bokkems)* drying in the wind up Saldanha and Lamberts Bay way you recapture Cape history, the men braving the seas, their women literally keeping the home fires burning: drying, salting and marketing the fish.

Fish pie can be delicious. Today we use any scraps of left-over fish dressed with a velvety mushroom sauce and topped with an instant potato topping to which we add one egg for colour and flavour. But here is the old Cape recipe:

Half fill a pie dish or casserole with seasoned flaked cooked fish and add any fishy things on hand, beaten strips of chokka (squid), oddments of rock lobster, a mussel or two, etc. Sprinkle the pie with grated cheese and/or buttered breadcrumbs and bake in a moderate oven for $^3/_4$ hour.

Cape Fish Bobotie

1 kg (2 lb) raw fish, minced (or fresh frozen fish), 2 slices of day-old bread (soaked in milk), 2 onions fried in butter and a little oil, 2 tablespoons curry powder (or to taste, depending on whether curry powder is mild or strong), juice of 1 lemon or 2 tablespoons vinegar, chopped and soaked peaches or apricots to taste (optional), or prepared apple rings (soaked), 2 eggs, 3 or 4 bay leaves (or 6 lemon leaves), 12 almonds, $^1/_2$ cup milk, salt, pepper and Knorr Aromat.

Mince the fish. Dip the bread in milk and squeeze the milk out. Cut the onion into thin slices, and fry in butter and oil until golden brown. Mix the curry powder, sugar, vinegar and salt. Add to the onion and cook a while. Add fish and 1 beaten egg and bread, and mix well. Put into a buttered dish, cover with well-beaten egg and milk. Decorate with almonds and lemon leaves. Bake over water until set.

Serve with prepared rice, slices of lemon, chutney and sambals to taste.

Fish Rissoles

Hilda's Old Dutch Way

> 500 g (1 lb) fresh or cooked fish, 1 onion fried in butter (chopped), 1 slice of soaked bread (squeezed dry), nutmeg, parsley, cayenne, salt, 2 eggs.

Mince the raw fish or flaked cooked fish with the chopped onion. Mix with the squeezed bread, seasoning and half the two beaten eggs. Roll in egg and fine breadcrumbs (or cracker crumbs) and fry in hot fat. Serve rissoles on a hot dish on a bed of mashed potatoes topped with a little melted butter and home made tomato sauce.

Preserved Roes for Garnishing

From an Old Cooking Guide

Take the roes of fresh salmon, cod or other large fish; wash them well to clear them from fibre and set them on a tin plate in a cool oven until quite dry. Beat them with a fork to separate the seeds, put the seeds into a bottle and store in a cool dry place. They will keep good for some time. A spoonful sprinkled lightly over any white fish will improve the appearance and taste.

Salting Carp

Free State Farmer's Wife's Method

Up-country people find carp a useful freshwater fish. It is comparable to any other type of fish if it has lived in healthy conditions. One farmer's wife told us she usually catches the carp in the afternoons, it is then cleaned, the head and intestines being discarded. After it has been well washed it is placed in a brine composed of a breakfast cup of salt dissolved in 5 litres (1 gallon) of cold water. It is important that the carp should remain in the brine overnight. The next morning it is taken out of the brine, seasoned to taste, then hung up in a cool place. After 5 hours it will be good for frying or may be curried.

Fresh Water Barbel

This ugly fish is a vegetarian and there is no reason why we shouldn't eat it. Chop off the head immediately when caught. Fry thick slices in hot fat after seasoning, with or without egg and breadcrumbs.

Trout Albany

> Trout, salt, pepper, $1/_4$ cup sour cream, seasoned flour, pinch sugar and Aromat, tablespoon each butter and oil.

Coat the trout in seasoned flour. Fry trout in mixture of butter and oil, turning as required. Add sour cream to sediment in pan and pour this sauce over. Garnish with fried almonds.

Shrimps, Prawns and Crawfish

When making sauce remember to use the shells and scraps of the shrimps or prawns by placing in a pan just covered with water. After tossing cooked shrimps in hot butter make a *roux* of the shrimp liquor with flour, boil and beat sauce well and pour over hot shrimps in hot sauceboat.

On Toothpicks

To serve prawns, cook them in their shells in salted water for about 20 minutes. Then remove the shell and the black vein down the back. Arrange them, each on a toothpick, on a dish with a mayonnaise dip, for guests to help themselves. The same applies to shrimps.

Crawfish (lobster) is usually served the same way. If you buy frozen tails, cook them in salted water, then remove and slit them down the soft part of the shell. Remove the meat and cut into chunks. Pierce each chunk with a toothpick and put back neatly into the shells. Mask with mayonnaise for guests to help themselves.

Oyster World

Generally speaking, on account of the high prices which they command nowadays, oysters are usually served on a plate in the half-shell, with cracked ice and home-made brown bread and butter, cayenne pepper and lemon wedges on the side. Oysters are also very good if put into a light batter and fried in deep oil for a few minutes. Two or three put into a beef stew or a beef pudding give a distinctive flavour, and in the nineteenth century, when they were very cheap, excellent soups and soufflés were made with oysters.

Batter for Two Dozen

1 cup flour, 1 cup milk, 1 egg, salt and pepper.

Make the batter by beating the egg and adding it to the flour, salt and pepper. Beat in the milk gradually, seeing that the batter is smooth. Use an egg-beater or a whisk to get rid of any lumps. Leave in a cool place for 30 minutes. Open and beard the oysters, then dip them in the batter and fry in deep hot, but not smoking, oil until they are golden brown. The oysters should not be over cooked. Serve hot with lemon wedges and the oyster juice.

Oysters Bredasdorp

Oysters, shrimps, mushrooms, flour, white wine, cream, cheese.

Half bake oysters on half shell. Make white wine sauce as follows: Chop one bunch shallots very finely. Fry in butter till brown. Add three tablespoons of flour and browning. Chop shrimp and mushrooms very finely, put in sauce with a glass of white wine and cream. Season to taste and allow to cook for 10 to 15 minutes. Pour sauce over oysters, covering with breadcrumbs and grated cheese, mixed. Put in oven to brown.

Oysters Brochette

12 oysters, 12 slices bacon.

Drain and wrap each oyster in a slice of bacon, using wooden toothpicks as skewers. Place in pan in oven at 180° C (350° F) and bake until bacon is done. Serve on toast.

Lesley's Oysters in Sherry Cream

To Serve Four

This is a quick, easy and impressive dish from Silwood Kitchen;

Heat a shallow casserole and in the meantime bring 1 cup of cream to boiling point then add $^1/_2$ cup sherry. Pour this sherry cream into the warm casserole and add 1 .2 litres (1 quart) well-drained fresh oysters; spread them out evenly and season well with salt and pepper, then cover with well-buttered breadcrumbs. Place in the oven under the grill just long enough to brown the breadcrumbs and heat the oysters until they curl at the edges. Serve with toast and a green salad and your favourite, moderately dry, white wine.

Mock Oysters

Using Salt Herring and Sweetbread

This recipe for mock oysters needs a herring and a sweetbread, and up to about a dozen deep oyster shells, well scrubbed and immaculately clean. Mince the flesh very finely of a herring (well soaked to extract salt), divide it into 12 parts putting one part into each of the oyster shells. Place upon each a piece of boiled sweetbread which has been dipped into egg and seasoned breadcrumbs. Now sprinkle more breadcrumbs over the mock oysters; top with a knob of butter and bake them in the oven. Serve very hot.

Fried Oysters

Pick over oysters, removing bits of shell and place in a colander to drain. Roll each oyster in seasoned Maizena (cornflour) and fry in deep hot fat, cooking only a few at a time, until brown. Drain on absorbent paper.

Octopus and Macaroni

This typical Greek dish is similar to Portuguese recipes for octopus.

250 g ($^1/_2$ lb) dry octopus, 500 g (1 lb) macaroni, 1 cup olive oil, 1 cup red wine, 1 cup fine cracker crumbs, 2 bay leaves, 2 tablespoons tomato paste, $^1/_2$ cup minced onion, 5 litres (4 quarts) water, salt, pepper, dill and parsley.

Soak the dry octopus overnight, and put through a meat chopper. Brown onion lightly in the oil, add the wine and the tomato paste, diluted in water. Add the octopus, salt and pepper. Simmer until the sauce thickens. In the meantime boil the macaroni in salted water. Drain. Place on a serving platter. Sprinkle with the cracker crumbs instead of the usual grated cheese and pour the sauce over. If fresh octopus is used it is finely chopped with a knife instead of being passed through a meat chopper.

Squid and Chokka

A Traditional Method

(The squid – *chokka* – is distinguished from the octopus by two extra arms, or tentacles.)

Slice the body part into thin slices about 5 cm (2″) or 7 .5 cm (3″) thick.

Now pass through flour, eggs and breadcrumbs and fry in deep oil or other fat. Beat the tentacles with a mallet and slice and cook them with vegetables. The resultant liquid is reduced and thickened and served with the fried pieces of chokka.

Perlemoen

Abalone, Klipkos

Skin divers (now strictly controlled) obtain perlemoen along the Cape West Coast. There are many ways of preparing and cooking it. (For further recipes write Silwood Kitchen, Rondebosch, C.P.) The following is our demonstration method.

Remove the abalone from the shell while still alive, if possible, but *do not* remove the beard, as the 'jell' is in this. Stun the fish by firm pressure of the thumb on the 'mouth', then slip the thumb or a blunt knife under the shallow side of the shell, i.e. opposite side to the holes, and ease the fish out of its shell.

Hammer sharply, with a kitchen mallet three or four times, to tenderise the fish. Remove the intestines and scrub the fish with a brush until there is no trace of the black slimy film. Do not cut the short tentacles off, as they have an exquisite flavour. (*Do not* allow salt or hot water near at this stage, as this will toughen the perlemoen.)

If using a pressure cooker, cook for 20 minutes in the following stock: 1 cup water and $^1/_2$ cup white wine.

If you do not have a pressure cooker, simmer gently in the above stock until tender when pierced with a skewer (about $1^1/_2$ hours).

Cut the perlemoen into cubes. Sauté in butter until lightly browned, then add its own liquid, and 1 or 2 tablespoons of white wine (to taste), a little grated nutmeg and finely-toasted breadcrumbs. Season well. Simmer until sauce reduces. Serve on a bed of cooked rice.

After cooking until tender as described above, the perlemoen can be minced and served in the sauce described above, or made into frikkadels (rissoles).

Curried Perlemoen

Trim shellfish into neat pieces, arrange in a fireproof dish, and cover with the curry sauce, prepared as follows: Fry a small clove of garlic, some minced spring onions, a teaspoon of grated coconut, a small tablespoon of curry powder, a teaspoon of tamarind* purée and a similar quantity of tomato purée. When nicely cooked, stir in a cup of yoghurt or cream, and add salt and pepper to taste; pour over the fish, and set for a few minutes in the oven, and serve quickly.

N.B. Never add salt or water to perlemoen when preparing it, else the result will be stringy, tasteless and tough.

* Obtainable from Indian stores

The Snail . . . Escargot

Our garden snail is said to have arrived in the Cape in 1854 when the French consul at Cape Town imported a barrel of live snails for his table. Some of the snails escaped, hence the plague of *Helix aspersa* in our gardens. As at the time of writing local fresh snails are not available commercially, those usually served are imported in tins. (Write Silwood Kitchen for recipes.)

The South African farmer's wife did not have it so easy when it came to rearing poultry – usually the woman's appointed task, while the menfolk took on the larger livestock. Records of life in the chicken run show that she was also kept on the run combating snakes and rooikats that invaded the hen-houses, and dosing when fowl sickness descended suddenly, often apparently when everything else was quiet. One bit of advice given in an old farming journal was to teach secretary birds to guard the poultry yard. These and geese being good 'watch-dogs'.

Today, of course chicken is one of our least expensive meats and, battery reared, does not require long simmering or that half cup of water in the roasting pan for tenderizing it. A moist stuffing or whole vegetables such as onion, orange, tomato inside, does increase tenderization of course.

Simple Roast Chicken

With Onion Stuffing

> 1 roasting chicken, 60 g (2 oz) mushrooms, 1 teaspoon paprika, egg to bind, 2 salad onions, 1 tomato, 60 g (2 oz) soft breadcrumbs, salt and pepper.

Skin the tomato and chop with the mushrooms and onion until fine. Mix all well together, add breadcrumbs, paprika, salt and pepper, and bind with a little egg. Push the stuffing into the cavity of the chicken, place it in roasting pan, cover with a piece of bacon, and roast in the usual way at 200° C (400° F), allowing 20 minutes to the pound. Serve with gravy from the roasting pan.

Cape Chicken

Traditional

This has a curried flavour and is served with salads and sambals such as chutney, banana and rice and sliced tomatoes sprinkled with finely chopped onion, shallots or chives.

Beat the breast and tender parts of chicken into flat pieces, spread with butter and roll. Marinate for twenty minutes in the following sauce:

> 4 tablespoons soya sauce, 2 tablespoons fresh grated ginger, 1 table-spoon curry powder.

Roll the marinated chicken and slice thinly then string on skewers and grill for three minutes over the fire.

Van Riebeeck Chicken Pie

As Served at Silwood Kitchen

> 1 chicken, 1 glass white wine, chicken stock, 1 chopped onion, mace and salt to taste, 12 peppercorns, $^1/_2$ teaspoon allspice, 2 tablespoons vermicelli, 1 tablespoon sago, 1 tablespoon butter.

Joint the chicken and put into a heavy bottomed pan with the onion. wine and stock to cover, and add the mace, peppercorns and allspice. Simmer for $^3/_4$ hour, then add the vermicelli, sago and butter. Stir continuously until thickened. Just before removing from the pan, add the yolk of an egg and the juice of $^1/_2$ a lemon. Allow it to get cold in a pie-dish, then place slices of hard-cooked egg on top of the chicken. Roll out puff pastry and make a cover; decorate as fancy dictates. Brush with beaten egg, and bake in a hot oven until brown.

Talking Turkey

Turkey for Christmas is decidedly not traditional to South Africa but it was revived by later British settlers and also by American immigrants who sought it for Thanksgiving. Goat, beef, lamb, suckling pig and venison featured on our old festive menus. Here, as briefly as we dare, are our demonstration methods for working with a turkey – not such hard work when you know how. But because space in this small book precludes many stuffings and further recipes for poultry, readers are invited to write for Silwood Kitchen's full repertoire. (Silwood Kitchen, Silwood Road, Rondebosch, Cape.)

Selecting a Turkey Today

Allow 250 g ($^1/_2$ lb) ready-to-cook weight per person per serving. The total cooking time for a 5 kg (10 lb) bird is 15 minutes to 500 g (1 lb) and 20 minutes more.

Thawing a Frozen Turkey: It is most important to see that your frozen turkey is completely thawed before cooking. Slow thawing is most satisfactory. Large turkeys will take two to three days to thaw in the bottom of the refrigerator. Remove from the refrigerator before cooking, so that flesh reaches room temperature. So have your frozen turkey delivered 2 or 3 days before Christmas Day, if you can. If you get landed with a frozen turkey at too short notice you can immerse it in warm water to speed up thawing.

Too Large for the Oven? It can happen. An old way out with a bird too big for your oven is to remove the legs and simmer these on top of the stove while the rest of the bird is roasted in the oven. For serving it is quite easy to fasten the legs with skewers; and if you brown them sufficiently no one is the wiser that the bird has been disjointed – as a matter of fact, it is easier to carve and the legs are all the more tender this way.

In the old days turkey was roasted on a spit over a clear fire with a piece of buttered paper protecting the breast and it was basted frequently. Today at Silwood Kitchen turkey is selected and roasted as follows:

Roast Turkey

1 turkey, pork sausages and celery for forcemeat (for the carcase), celery, apricot and walnut stuffing (for the breast), 185 g–250 g (6–8 oz) butter or margarine – sufficient to cover bird, about 600 ml (1 pint) well flavoured stock, 1 rounded tablespoon flour to thicken gravy, salt, pepper and Aromat.

For garnish: 250 g (8 oz) rashers of streaky bacon, watercress, 500 g (1 lb) chipolata sausages, 1 can cranberry sauce or amatingulu jelly. (For latter refer to *Index.*)

Set oven 180° C (350° F). Prepare the forcemeat and stuffing. Undo trussing string from turkey legs, if necessary, and put the forcemeat into the carcass through the vent end. Re-tie trussing string. Loosen neck skin and push second stuffing well into breast cavity. Pull skin gently over stuffing and fasten under wing tips. A skewer can be pushed in to hold it firm. Put turkey in the roasting tin.

Spread butter thickly over a double sheet of greaseproof paper or sheet of foil. Lay the buttered sheet over bird and pour round half the stock. Turn and baste bird about every 20 minutes, but keep paper or foil on while cooking. If stock reduces too much during cooking, add a little more. After 1 hour, cut trussing string holding legs. Just before bird is cooked, prepare the garnish. Remove rind from bacon rashers, and wash and trim watercress. Grill bacon rashers and sausages.

To test if the bird is cooked pierce thigh with a skewer, if clear juice runs out, not pink, the bird is ready. Once cooked, set turkey on serving dish, pull out trussing strings and skewer, garnish with bacon rashers, sausages and watercress, then keep warm.

If bird is not sufficiently brown towards the end of cooking time, remove paper and leave bird until golden-brown.

To make gravy: strain juices from roasting tin into a saucepan and deglaze tin with remaining stock. Add this stock to juices and skim off some of the fat. Put fat back into tin, stir in flour, then pour in liquid from saucepan. Stir until boiling. Season and strain back into saucepan. When ready to serve, reheat gravy and serve it separately.

Celery and Sausage Stuffing

For the Carcase

> 3–4 sticks celery, 1 onion, 15 g ($^1/_2$ oz) butter, 1 teaspoon mixed herbs, salt, pepper, Aromat, pinch of sugar, about 370 g (12 oz) sausage meat.

This should be sufficient for an average size turkey. Chop celery and onion finely. Place them in frypan with the butter, mixed herbs and seasonings. Cook slowly for 2–3 minutes. When cooked combine with the sausage meat.

Celery, Apricot and Walnut Stuffing

For the Breast

> 2 small sprigs of celery (thinly sliced), 125 g (4 oz) dried apricots (soaked overnight), 250 g (8 oz) walnuts (chopped), 3 tablespoons butter, 4 onions (chopped), 3 cups fresh breadcrumbs, 2 tablespoons parsley (chopped), salt and pepper.

Drain apricots and cut each half into 3–4 pieces. Melt butter in a pan, add onions, cover and cook until soft. Then add celery, apricots and walnuts. Cook about 4 minutes over a brisk heat, stirring continuously, then turn into a bowl. When cool, add crumbs and parsley. Season to taste.

Rice and Bacon Stuffing

Cook 1 cup parboiled rice. Fry 6 rashers of bacon until crisp. Remove from pan. Chop finely 1 large onion and cook in bacon fat until transparent; add bacon, onion, bacon fat, $^1/_2$ teaspoon mixed herbs, salt, pepper, Aromat and a pinch of sugar to the cooked rice. This makes 5 cups full.

Roast Duckling

Stuff, truss and roast in the oven – preferably in a covered basting pan – if liked on a bed of bacon. Remove the cover to brown and crispen the bird. Allow 40 minutes roasting time for a bird $1^1/_4$ kg ($2^1/_2$ lb) in a moderate oven.

Duck Glazed with Apricots

Great Grandmama used fruits to give piquancy to certain meats. Apricots, dried and fresh were particularly prized for stuffing hams and also for glamorizing duck. Here is a change from the usual *duck l'orange* adapted from an old recipe.

> 1 large tin canned apricots, 1 tablespoon lemon juice, juice and rind of 1 orange, 1 teaspoon ginger, 1 teaspoon soy sauce, a pinch of salt, pepper and MSG.

Bring the above ingredients to the boil and simmer for 15 minutes. Strain and pour sauce over the roasted duck, which must be well drained from all fat before you cloak it with the sauce. Reduce oven heat and allow to glaze without browning.

Silwood's Salmi of Wild Duck

> 2 wild ducks, 2 wineglasses of port wine, $^1/_2$ cup of stock, 6 shallots, juice of one Seville orange, salt, pepper and a dash of cayenne.

Half roast the wild ducks and cut them up. Put a glass of wine and the stock, the shallots chopped finely, the fruit juice and the seasoning into a pan over a low flame, and simmer together for 5 minutes to amalgamate, then add the second glass of wine. When it boils, add the jointed wild ducks. Test for seasoning, and allow to simmer until quite tender. Total cooking time is about 45 minutes. Serve with green beans and creamed potatoes.

To Cook Your Goose

Traditional with Apples Inside

The most popular way of dealing with a fully-grown goose, before and at Christmas time, is to roast it whole. For a goose weighing approximately 5 kg (10 lb) you need salt, pepper, a little marjoram, a pinch of crushed caraway seeds, approximately 750 g ($1^1/_2$ lb) of small sweet apples (not cooking apples), and a little butter.

Rub the inside of the cleaned goose with salt, pepper and marjoram and crushed caraway seeds, the outside with salt and pepper. Wash, dry and core the apples. Do not peel them. Put apples inside the goose. To extract as much fat as possible from the goose, roast it slowly, at 170° C (325° F), allowing at least fifteen minutes' cooking time to $^1/_2$ kg (1 lb). Cover the goose with lightly-buttered foil and put it on a grid in a deep roasting tin. Baste it with its own fat. Halfway through the cooking pour off the fat from the tin. Save the fat for cooking. To brown the goose nicely all over, remove the foil half an hour before the goose is cooked. The drumstick should be soft when bird is done. Leave the goose to rest for at least ten minutes before carving. Pour off all fat from the roasting tin. Make a little gravy with wine, or stock, but no thickening.

A goose is excellent roasted on the spit, if you have a big enough spit. Our German settlers serve roast goose with apples (cooked inside), a white or red cabbage, or sauerkraut cooked with wine and dumplings or potatoes. Like hot roast pork, goose is sometimes accompanied by a hot cabbage salad. Roasted pototoes go well with goose.

Roast Goose

With Orange Ginger Glaze

Orange and ginger glaze balances the richness of roast goose. Serve some of the orange slices with each portion.

> 1 goose, weighing 4 kg–6 kg (8–12 lb), salt, pepper, Knorr Aromat, 1 onion (cut in pieces), several stalks celery (cut in pieces), 1 or 2 apples (cut in pieces), watercress or parsley, orange slices.

Sprinkle the cavity of the goose with salt, pepper and Knorr Aromat. Fill the cavity with the onion, celery, and apple pieces. Close the neck and abdominal openings with skewers. Place on a rack in a roasting pan. Roast in a moderately slow oven at 170° C (325° F) until internal temperature reaches 82° C (180° F), or until drumstick moves easily. Baste frequently during last 40 minutes with orange ginger glaze until all the glaze is used. Decorate serving platter with watercress or parsley and orange slices. Yield: 6–8 servings.

Orange Ginger Glaze

> $^3/_4$ cup orange marmalade, $^1/_2$ cup port wine or cider, 1 tablespoon wine vinegar, 2 tablespoons crystallized ginger, (finely chopped).

Blend together in a small saucepan the orange marmalade, port wine or cider, vinegar and ginger. Heat until simmering, stirring occasionally.

Ostrich Country

One of the most popular tourist attractions is a visit to a show farm at Oudtshoorn where every schoolboy must try riding an ostrich and where venturesome adults, too, get a kick out of it – that is,. by avoiding those fearsome ones from the bird. The famous Cango Caves nearby complete what must be one of the most unusual holidays anywhere in the world.

In the Oudtshoorn district ostrich eggs are used for daily eating, for omelettes and cakes, and the flesh of the ostrich is also used for making biltong and many meat dishes. (Futher recipes for using ostrich eggs in cakes and the making of biltong from ostrich meat may be obtained from Silwood Kitchen, Rondebosch, Cape.)

Roasted Ostrich

Silwood Kitchen made history when an ostrich was roasted for the occasion of the opening of its branch at Inanda Johannesburg in 1974. Any reader sufficiently ambitious to tackle this task is invited to write **Lesley Faull** (Silwood Kitchen, Rondebosch, C.P.) for all the details. In meantime here are two traditional and well tested recipes from Silwood.

Roast Leg of Ostrich

Served with Glazed Quinces

4 kg (8 lb) ostrich leg.

Marinade: 1 sliced carrot, 1 sliced onion, 1 clove garlic, cut very small, 2 bay leaves, 3 or 4 cloves, ground black pepper, red wine to almost cover, lemon leaves, 1 teaspoon fennel, pinch thyme, 1 teaspoon tarragon vinegar, peel of $^1/_2$ an orange.

Marinate the meat for 24 to 48 hours. First pour a little oil on top to prevent meat from going black. When required, drain the liquid and brown the meat in a mixture of oil and butter. Add two tomatoes, peeled and cut into small pieces, 1 level tablespoon flour and salt. Add liquid again. Place in a heavy iron pot and roast for one hour at 180° C (350° F) for a further hour.

Serve with glazed quinces, sweet potatoes and yellow rice and raisins.

Glazed Quinces

Accompaniment for Pork or Ostrich

1 kg (2 lb) quinces, dried naartjie peel, 3 tablespoons butter, stick cinnamon, 1 cup brown sugar,

Peel and slice the quinces. Wash in salted water. Place fruit in a heavy-bottomed saucepan together with the naartjie peel, butter, stick cinnamon, brown sugar, salt, and 1 small cup of water. Simmer gently and when quinces are cooked, and the water has boiled away, increase the heat and fry to a golden colour. Remove cinnamon and naartjie peel before serving.

Braised Ostrich Oudtshoorn

Ostrich meat should be treated like venison and marinated. We like to layer it in 2 cartons of drinking yoghurt for six to eight days, turning the meat every day.

1 kg (2 lb) ostrich meat, 2 cartons of drinking yoghurt, sunflower oil, 125 g ($^1/_4$ lb) button onions, 1 medium onion (sliced), 2 medium carrots (chopped), 1 green sweet pepper (chopped), 1 red sweet pepper (chopped), 1 tablespoon flour, 2 cups stock, 1 cup Witzenberg Rivoli, salt and pepper, Aromat, pinch of sugar, 125 g ($^1/_4$ lb) mushrooms, a handful of prunes, de-pipped and stuffed with almonds.

Take the meat out of the yoghurt, wash off and dry. Then cut it into squares. Heat a heavy bottomed saucepan with sufficient oil to cover base, and when hot fry pieces of meat briskly until brown on both sides. Take meat out of saucepan and sauté button onions until brown, remove and reserve. Add sliced onion, chopped carrots and peppers. Fry more slowly until beginning to get colour. Draw off the heat. Pour off surplus fat, leaving one tablespoon. Stir in flour. Cook slowly for a minute or two, then add stock, bring to boil, add wine and season. Replace the meat. Cover, simmering gently on stove top or in oven at 130° C (250° F) for 2–3 hours until the meat is tender. Fifteen minutes before serving add the mushrooms, sautéed onions and prunes. Adjust seasoning and spoon into a hot casserole for serving.

Pigeons

Students of architecture delight in the pigeon houses that form part of the peaceful scene in so many gardens of old Cape homes. Pigeons, stewed, fried and pied were popular in those old days and many are the recipes. The old Malayan recipe included here reflects some feeling for the birds, even in those days; but at Silwood Kitchen co-author Lesley complains her husband Dr George Faull is so fond of his carrier birds none are available for the pot.

Advice from Silwood Kitchen

Keep pigeons for at least a week in the refrigerator as they are inclined to be tough if cooked too soon. Stuff pigeons in the usual way or with a rasher of bacon. Place two tablespoons of butter or oil in a rosting pot. Roll the pigeons in seasoned flour and brown lightly, turning frequently. Add boiling water and let the pigeons simmer in this gravy. A few allspice will give a piquant flavour. When the pigeons are tender add $^1/_8$ cup of dry wine for each pigeon. Serve whole. Garnish with parsley.

Silwood's Braised Pigeon

Clean pigeons and wipe with a damp cloth. Dry and flour lightly. Chop up 1 onion; put 2 tablespoons butter or oil in heavy saucepan or casserole, and fry onion until golden brown. Remove onion. Brown the pigeons in the hot fat. Add more oil if necessary. Remove pigeons and set aside with onion. Add 2 heaped tablespoons of flour to oil. Stir continuously. When a dark brown, slowly add 600 ml (1 pint) stock (or chicken cube dissolved in water), salt, $^1/_2$ teaspoon freshly ground pepper, 1 tablespoon soy sauce or other seasoning. Cook sauce for about 5 minutes. Put a strip of bacon round each pigeon. Place carefully in sauce, add $^1/_2$ cup red wine. Cover and cook slowly in the oven at 130° C (250° F). After an hour remove and baste the pigeons. Add more wine if liquid is too thick. Add 1 teaspoon sugar. Replace in the oven and cook for 1 hour longer. Remove. Season to taste. Serve with plain steamed rice and apple jelly.

Fried Pigeons Cooked with Honey

This is an old Malayan recipe that finds favour with those who keep pigeons and occasionally cull a few for the pot.

Before killing, intoxicate the pigeons with a little alcohol as this improves the flesh and is kinder to the birds. After killing the birds, cleaning and dressing them, rub the inside of each with salt and aniseed, then all over the outside, coat with thinned honey. (Place honey in a pot of hot water to make this easier.) Heat some oil until very hot and fry the pigeons until tender and a really rich brown. After draining break them apart to serve, sprinkling well with pepper.

Jugged Pigeons and Squabs

3 squabs, or 4 plump wood pigeons, 2 onions (sliced), 300 ml ($^1/_2$ pint) brown ale, or cider, bouquet garni, 300 ml ($^1/_2$ pint) good stock, kneaded butter, squeeze of lemon, parsley for garnishing.

Stuffing: 2 hard-cooked eggs, 1 cup fresh breadcrumbs, 2 tablespoons shredded suet, pigeons' liver, good pinch of ground mace, 2 tablespoons chopped mixed herbs and parsley, 1 small egg (beaten), salt and pepper. Knorr Aromat.

Set oven at 170° C–180° C (325° F–350° F). First prepare the stuffing; push the yolks of the hard -cooked eggs through a strainer and add to the crumbs with the suet. Reserve the whites. Blanch and chop the livers and add to the yolk mixture with the mace, herbs and sufficient beaten egg to moisten; add the seasonings. Wipe the pigeons and stuff them with the mixture. Truss them and pack into a thick casserole with the onions. Pour over the ale (or cider), add the bouquet garni and half the stock. Bring to the boil, then put in pre-set slow to moderate oven for 1–2$^1/_2$ hours (1 hour for squabs, longer for wood pigeons) or until very tender.

Tip off the gravy into another pan and remove bouquet garni. Thicken the gravy with the kneaded butter and add rest of the stock if necessary. (There should be about 300–425 ml ($^1/_2$–$^3/_4$ pint) of gravy in all.) Add a squeeze of lemon and bring to the boil. If using squabs, take up and cut in half, first removing string Leave the wood pigeons whole but remove string. Pour over the gravy and serve in the casserole. Shred the reserved egg white, scatter it over the top and sprinkle with parsley.

Pigeon Pie – Legs Up

Hilda's 'Where Is It' Recipe

> 4 young pigeons, pepper, salt, gravy, 1 glass wine, 60 g (2 oz) butter, a few slices of ham, slices of hard-boiled egg, 1 cup of good stock (or chicken cubes and water).

Lay a rim of paste round the sides and edges of a piedish. After the pigeons are cleaned, halve them; add other ingredients and liquid and season as you would any other pie. Cover with puff paste; ornament the top and stick four of the little feet out of it. Brush over with egg and milk, bake for an hour and a half with buttered paper over the crust to prevent its burning.

Note: We prefer to place the pie in a very hot oven to bake the crust, then reduce heat until birds are tender. As for those little feet maybe they should be covered with foil!

Braised Grouse

> 2 grouse, fat bacon, parsley, pepper, 2 slices of raw ham, 2 onions, 2 stalks of celery, 300 ml ($^1/_2$ pint) of bouillon.

Chop the livers with a thick slice of bacon, add minced parsley, season with pepper, and put inside the bird. Heat a little fat in a pan and cook the chopped ham and vegetables until soft but not coloured. Add some of the bouillon, lay the grouse on top, pour on the rest of the bouillon, cover and simmer gently for about 1$^1/_2$ hours. Remove surplus fat and serve with an onion purée.

Partridge

Partridges were so abundant that they often afforded 'a very agreeable repast' as recorded in our oldest books. Partridge is best simply roasted. Cover the breast of the bird with a thick rasher of fat bacon or pork. Work a knob of butter up with some salt and pepper and a teaspoon of lemon juice and put this inside the bird. Roast for 20–25 minutes in a fairly hot oven. Serve with a good pan gravy, fried breadcrumbs, potato straws or crisps, and a green salad.

Partridge Provencale

2 partridges, fat bacon 60 g (2 oz) of butter, 1 clove of garlic, 60 g (2 oz) of mushrooms, a glass of dry white wine.

Wrap each bird in a thin fat rasher and braise in butter. Add one clove of garlic, chopped finely. Put on the lid and cook very gently for about 25 minutes, then remove to a dish and keep hot. Add the sliced mushrooms to the pan and, when they are cooked, pour in a glass of dry white wine. Bring to the boil, allow to reduce a little, lay the partridges on top and finish cooking over a slow heat for a few minutes until the birds are quite tender.

Guinea Fowl

Guinea fowl require to be well larded and simmered, using a similar method to the tough fowls of yesteryear.

Guinea Fowl with Wine

1 guinea fowl, 3 cups dry white wine, 125 g ($^1/_4$ lb) butter, salt and pepper, 125 g ($^1/_4$ lb) bacon (diced), 250 ml (1 cup) thin beef stock, 1 bouillon cube.

Marinate the guinea fowl for about 3 days in the wine. Turn every 12 hours. Melt butter in a casserole dish. Add the guinea fowl, which has been allowed to drain. Cook until golden brown, turning occasionally. Sprinkle with salt and pepper. Add the bacon, which should be cut into small squares and the rind removed. Pour the stock over and the wine in which the bird was marinated. Simmer gently for just over two hours, in a moderate oven. Serve with quince or red currant jelly.

Roast Pheasant

A young bird, thick slice of fat pork or bacon, 60 g (2 oz) butter, seasoning, 1 teaspoon lemon juice.

Tie the piece of fat meat over the breast of the bird, or lard it with strips of the fat. Season the butter with salt, pepper, and lemon juice and put inside the bird. Place in a well-greased roasting tin and roast in a moderate oven for about 30 minutes. Remove the fat from the breast, dredge with flour, baste with a little of the melted butter and allow the bird to brown, taking a further 15–25 minutes according to size. Serve with a good pan gravy, fried bread-crumbs, straw potatoes, bread sauce and green beans or a salad.

Casserole of Old Pheasant or Guinea Fowl

An old pheasant, 4 large onions, 3 tablespoons butter, a slice of fat bacon or pork, 2 tablespoons flour, $^1/_2$ cup white wine or stock.

Peel and slice the onions and lay them in the bottom of a deep casserole. Tie the fat meat over the breast of the bird, melt the butter in a pan, and brown the bird all over. Remove it and lay it on top of the onions, cover tightly and cook in a moderate oven for an hour. Remove the bird from the casserole, stir in the flour, allowing it to brown, then add the white wine or stock. Replace the bird, cover and continue cooking for a further 30 minutes or until tender. Serve in the casserole.

Golden Plovers
With Grapes

> 4 plovers, 125 g (4 oz) of small seedless white grapes, butter, 4 slices of toast.

Stuff the plovers with the grapes and roast in butter, basting well, for about 15 minutes. Butter the toast, and place a bird on each piece. Serve plain or with a little pan gravy.

Entomophagy
The Eating of Insects

The eating of insects is not foreign to South Africans, White or Black. Locusts that consume the sweetest crops could be eaten out of sweet vengeance as well as for their taste. Today, of course locusts are eaten with caution, for they might have been sprayed with poison. However, if you must know how Africans and Europeans enjoyed locusts in the past – they removed the heads and the last joint of the hind legs, then roasted them and ate them with salt. Or alternatively the roasted locusts were ground to a fine powder and mixed with wild honey – as did John the Baptist!

Ants – Rysmiere

According to Lawrence Green *(Karoo)* you approach the ant-heap with a *rys-yster* a flat piece of iron which gives out a dull sound if the ants are home. After rain, as a rule, satisfactory hauls of ants are made. Another almost infallible sign is the budding of the *'ngomsganna* plant. The edible ants are not the ordinary inhabitants of the ant-heap; they are the young king and queen ants which forsake the heap on wings. Having secured your rysmiere, throw them into lukewarm water and they will float. Other ants, which may be mixed with them, which are not so salty, will sink. Dry the *rysmiere* in the wind and grill in a frying-pan. The abundant fat given out is Namaqualand's most valued ointment for sores, bruises and burns.

How do you serve grilled ants? Spread them on bread and butter.

Ants and Bushman Rice

The larvae of ants is another delicacy known to the old-timers of Namaqualand, obviously learnt from the Bushmen who opened ant heaps and took out the white pupae and roasted it on hot stones.

Termite farming has been discussed seriously at Government level. Experiments in Rhodesia showed that the proteins-per-acre yield from termites is five times that of ordinary cattle.

✻ ✻ ✻

Picnics

A picnic at the Fresh River was a treat for Van Riebeeck's children and their friends although fraught with anxiety for the parents. There was always fear lest a child strayed, as lions prowled, snakes lurked in the bush, and one could never trust the Hottentots who had a penchant for stealing the brass buttons off the children's clothes. (Just, as in the same way, the children of British settlers 200 years later were in danger from Africans who coveted their pearl buttons. African bead work in our museums embellished with pearl buttons of that period – bear witness to those buttons bartered for or torn from the clothes as occasion offered.)

eat & Game

and Savoury Dishes

Maybe the first meat the Van Riebeecks ate ashore was from a hippo. After 19 days aboard the flagship *Dromedaris* in the Bay, Van Riebeeck brought his family ashore to occupy the wooden shed his men had prepared for them inside the area allocated for the fort. It was on this day April 24, 1652 that a hippopotamus was killed and the meat declared to be good eating. One can imagine the men sitting round a rough table eating hippo steaks garnished with sorrel from the mountainside and the women, as was customary, eating from their laps, after grace. Van Riebeeck fined those who ate 'like pigs' and who did not precede food with grace.

The Braai Tradition

The third edition of our book *Braai and Barbecue* (1974) covers this subject, from the roasting of an ox to general camping fare and entertaining accompaniments. Suitable food for braaing will be found in the *Index* at the end of this book under, Boerewors, Breads, Chops, Drinks, Fish, Fruits, Meat Loaf, Marinades, Putu, Skewer foods, Soutribbetjies, Sosaties, Steak and Vegetables.

With a Grill Your Reputation is at Stake

When planning a grill the home cook knows that her reputation is at stake. The steak should not be too fresh, so why not 'copy-cat' the steak houses who mature their steaks for some days? The lower part of the refrigerator will serve for this. And another secret – never add the salt until the steak has almost finished cooking. The thicker the steak, the more succulent it will be.

To Grill Steak: Brush grid and steak with butter or salad oil. Season the steak with pepper (no salt), and break down the tissues by banging with a rolling pin or steak mallet. Or marinade the meat by leaving it to stand for an hour in a mixture of oil and vinegar to which seasoning has been added, such as a pinch each of sugar, garlic salt, MSG or Zeal and a crushed clove of garlic. (Several marinades appear in our book *Braai and Barbecue in Southern Africa*.). Place the prepared steak on the grid of the grill pan with the vegetables – tomatoes, mushrooms, and so on – on the bottom of the pan. Grill the meat rapidly on either side, turning once only; this will produce the rare (underdone) steak enjoyed by so many people; but if the steak is to be better done, lower the heat, or place lower down to finish the grilling. Add salt only when serving.

To Fry Steak: Cook large steaks in hot, shallow oil or butter mixed with oil, very quickly to brown both sides and seal the surface, then reduce heat to complete the cooking, turning again. Small steaks are best cooked on one side for half the time, then turned only once.

Cooking Time for Steaks

	Rare	Medium Rare	Well Done
18 mm (³/₄″) thick	5 mins.	9–10 mins.	14–15 mins.
25 mm (1″) thick	6–7 mins.	10 mins.	15 mins.
36 mm (1¹/₂″) thick	10 mins.	12–14 mins.	18–20 mins.

Tenderising Steak with Papaw Leaves

The traditional way to make steak tender was to use papaw leaves and many country people still do this in the following way:

Take a few papaw leaves and crush them in the hands. Bruise the steak with a rolling-pin in the usual way, then lay some of the bruised leaves under and on top of the meat. Press the whole slightly to ensure contact of leaves and meat and leave for about 7 minutes. Remove the leaves and cook as usual.

Sausages

Sausages should be lightly pricked and grilled slowly until well done inside and a golden brown on the outside. They may be brushed with oil for grilling.

A favourite method of ours is to dip the sausages in milk and then into seasoned flour before frying in a little fat. They don't burst this way and will be crisp and tasty – and, incidentally, go further.

Boerewors

To get the best results from Boerewors do not prick it, but steam or simmer the entire coiled sausage in a little water in a pan. (This may be done in advance at home.) Grill to a golden brown, cutting to the length required as you serve it.

Boerewors

To Make it at Home

1¹/₂ kg (3 lb) mutton, 1¹/₂ kg (3 lb) pork, 1¹/₂ kg (3 lb) beef, 750 g (1¹/₂ lb) tail fat, 750 g (1¹/₂ lb) pork fat.

Mince all the ingredients except the fat, which should be cut into tiny cubes and added last to the minced meat. To the mince mixture now add 2 tablespoons vinegar, 2 tablespoons salt, 1 tablespoon pepper, 4 tablespoons ground coriander, 1 dessertspoon ground cloves, 1 tablespoon allspice. Mix seasoning well with mince and fill sausage skins.

Skewered Foods

Today in South Africa traditional skewered meats that have survived from our past are the sosaties (marinated in curry and spices) and the kebabs, non-curried pieces of food impaled on skewers, often with pieces of fruit as well as meat. The skewers are available in hardware stores.

Sosatie and rice was such a favourite of the old Cape days that a number of wayside eating shops existed where this dish only was served. Not even a cup of coffee or tea was given with it, unless specially ordered. This may seem strange to us today, but an old Capetonian assured us that when mealtimes came round it took the proprietors all their time frying fast enough to supply their customers! Beef can be used for sosaties as well, but the right meat is a leg of mutton.

Sosaties

To Ensure Juicy Shish Kebab

When lamb is marinated for shish kebab, the juices frequently run out and the meat becomes tough and dry when cooked. Here is the remedy: Compensate for the fat deficiency. If no oil is used in the marinade, add a small quantity of a bland oil or olive oil. However, the marinade needs no oil if the cubes of meat are brushed well with butter or oil before they are broiled. And make certain that the meat is broiled under high heat. A low temperature will also cause drying and toughening of the meat.

Sosaties (1)

$1^1/_2$ kg (3 lb) de-boned leg of lamb with fat, membranes and tendons removed, all cut into 5 cm (2'') cubes.

Marinade: 1 cup chopped onion, 1 cup pale dry sherry, $^1/_4$ cup sunflower oil, 2 teaspoons oregano, 1 teaspoon thyme, 1 teaspoon salt, black pepper to taste, Knorr Aromat (MSG), $^1/_4$ teaspoon sugar, $1^1/_2$ garlic clove (minced), pineapple pieces or prunes, baby onions, rice.

Sprinkle the meat well with Knorr Aromat. Mix all the ingredients for the sauce in a shallow dish and immerse the meat cubes in marinade for eight hours for the best results. Then thread cubes of meat, pineapple pieces or prunes and parboiled baby onions on skewers. Grill until well browned. Serve on a bed of hot Armenian rice.

Armenian Rice and Egg Noodles

6 tablespoons butter and a few drops oil, $^1/_2$ cup small egg noodles, $1^1/_2$ cups American long grain rice, 1 teaspoon salt, 3 cups boiling water 1 beef stock cube.

Heat 6 tablespoons butter and a few drops of oil (to prevent burning) in a heavy-bottomed pan. Add $^1/_2$ cup uncooked small egg noodles, stir constantly until golden brown. Add $1^1/_2$ cups American long grain rice, stir constantly until rice is butter-coated. Add 1 teaspoon salt and 3 cups of boiling water, to which 1 beef stock cube has been added. Cook 20 minutes until water has been absorbed.

Sosaties (2)

1 fat leg of lamb or mutton, 2 tablespoons ground coriander, $^1/_2$ teaspoon cinnamon, 1 teaspoon ground ginger, 1 teaspoon ground allspice, $^1/_4$ teaspoon ground cardamon, 2 teaspoons salt, $^1/_4$ teaspoon pepper, Knorr Aromat, 3 large onions, 1 cup dried apricots and peaches, $^1/_2$ cup white wine vinegar, 1 cup red wine, 12 lemon leaves (bruised to get all the flavour out), 1 tablespoon brown sugar, curry to taste.

To prepare the meat: Mix all the spices together. Cut the leg into 3 .5 cm ($1^1/_2''$) cubes, cutting away all sinews. Slice onions 6 mm ($^1/_4''$) thick. Cut fruits into halves. Mix all the dry ingredients together. Combine the wine and vinegar. Pack a layer of meat into an earthenware basin, then a layer of onion. Sprinkle with spices and follow with the vinegar mixture. Repeat the process until all the meat has been used up. Pour over remaining spices and vinegar and leave to marinate for 36–48 hours. Turn once during that time. Take out meat and re-heat the liquid to serve as a sauce.

Soak the apricots and peaches for one to two hours. Slice some extra onion 6 mm ($^1/_4''$) thick. Pack in layers on sticks or skewers; meat, onion, apricot, peach, meat, onion, apricot, etc., and grill slowly.

Chicken Liver Kebabs (1)

Seasoning, 185 g (6 oz) chicken livers, oil or butter, 4 thin slices white bread, 3 tomatoes, chopped fresh parsley, small packet of stuffing.

Season livers. Seal in hot oil or melted butter. Remove crusts from bread, cut each slice into 3 or 4 fingers. Wrap one around each liver. Quarter tomatoes, roll in parsley. Make up stuffing mix, form into small forcemeat balls. Put livers, tomatoes and forcemeat balls on to 4 long skewers. Brush with oil, grill for 5–6 minutes.

Chicken Liver Kebabs (2)

With Bacon and Mushrooms

Chicken livers, rashers of bacon, olives, mushroom caps, stoneless prunes, soaked overnight in water, melted butter, dry breadcrumbs, seasoning.

Wrap livers in bacon. Arrange all ingredients alternately on skewers. Brush with melted butter, season well and toss in breadcrumbs. Grill for about 6 minutes or until cooked.

Frankfurter and Peach Kebabs

Frankfurters, canned peach halves, cherries, mushroom caps.

Arrange all ingredients alternately on skewers. Brush with melted butter and grill for 8 minutes.

Kebabs with Eggs

Truly Malay

1 kg (2 lb) mince meat, $^1/_3$ loaf of white bread, 2–3 eggs, a piece of butter, some grated nutmeg, a few bay leaves, 2 finely chopped onions, 2 cloves garlic.

Pound together the onions, garlic, pepper and some salt and then mix all the ingredients together except the bay leaves. Put the mixture into a large basin. Take a few pieces of live wood-coal and put them on the meat. Cover the dish with a cloth to keep the smoke inside. After a little while, remove the cloth. Have ready some hard-cooked eggs. Take a little of the meat mixture and fold it round the egg so that the egg is quite covered. Heat a little oil in a pan, and add the bay leaves. Then fry all the kebabs until they are done.

You must baste them while they fry, otherwise they will be dry. The fat should not be too hot. When they are all done, cut up some more onions and brown them in a little more fat. Flavour the onions with tamarind juice, sugar and salt. They must be pleasantly sweet-sour. Pile the onions on the kebabs, and serve them with lots of nice dry rice.

Liver in Caul Fat

Skilpad (1)

Here are two recipes for this very old farm favourite which makes an excellent 'extra' for your braaivleis.

1 sheep's liver (all skin and tubes removed), a thick slice of bread, 2 tablespoons chutney, 2 tablespoons sultanas or raisins (without pips) 2 tablespoons vinegar or $^1/_2$ tablespoon lemon juice, $^1/_2$ teaspoon baking powder, salt, pepper, cloves, allspice to taste.

Mince the liver, add bread well crumbed, then add all other ingredients. Mix well and place the mixture in the caul fat. Fold over and secure with toothpicks. Braai, bake or fry.

Skilpad (2)

1 sheep's liver (minced with the thin flank of the sheep), 1 chopped onion, 1 tablespoon grape vinegar, 1–2 eggs, 1 cup breadcrumbs, 1 tablespoon curry powder *or* 2 tablespoons tomato sauce.

Mix all ingredients and place in a sheep's caul. Fold into a neat parcel, put in a roasting pan and bake in a moderate oven for about an hour or until the juices run clear. Do not overcook.

Soutribbetjies for Braai-ing

2 kg (4 lb) of mutton, 250 g ($^1/_2$ lb) salt, 1 tablespoon natural brown sugar and $^1/_2$ teaspoon saltpetre.

Mix, then rub salt, sugar and saltpetre into the ribs and leave in an earthenware dish for 2 days. Then hang up the ribs to dry. Place ribs in a saucepan of cold water and simmer until the meat is tender. Grill the ribs on a greased wire griller over the coals until done. Serve hot or cold with green salad.

Steak and Beer Special

1 kg (2 lb) stewing steak, 250 g ($^1/_2$ lb) bacon, 1 large onion, 2 tablespoons apple, guava or red currant jelly, 600 ml (1 pint) beer, MSG, 1 bouillon cube.

Fry the chopped onion until soft. Add the cut-up bacon. Cook and remove to the side of the pan while browning the meat, which has been coated with seasoned flour (use MSG *not* salt). Place the meat, bacon and onion in a casserole, add the jelly and bouillon cube to the beer, and pour over the meat mixture. Put on the lid and cook in a slow oven at 140° C (250° F) until tender. Serve topped with croûtons of fried bread.

Accompaniments are prepared parboiled rice, peas and a green salad.

Old Fashioned Boiled Beef

Short ribs of beef $2^1/_2$–3 kg (5–6 lb), 1 onion, 2 carrots, 2 celery stalks, 3 parsley sprigs.

Into a large soup pot put $2^1/_2$ litres (2 quarts) of water. Add the meat which has been cut into good sized pieces when the water boils. Add the seasonings and 2 teaspoons of salt. Boil this for $2^1/_2$ hours. Remove meat from water and before serving be sure to remove the bone. Serve with tomato horse-radish sauce.

Tomato Horseradish Sauce

$^1/_2$ cup tomato ketchup, 2 teaspoons horseradish, 1 teaspoon vinegar, $^1/_4$ teaspoon salt.

Mix these ingredients together and chill until ready to use with boiled beef.

Meat Loaf Twist

This meat loaf looks like a Swiss roll and the filling consists of green pepper, celery and mushrooms.

$^1/_2$ cup green peppers (chopped), $^1/_2$ cup celery (chopped), $^1/_2$ cup fresh mushrooms (sliced), a little butter for frying, 750 g ($1^1/_2$ lb) minced beef, $^3/_4$ cup rolled or instant oats (uncooked), $1^1/_2$ teaspoons salt, $^1/_4$ teaspoon pepper, $^1/_2$ teaspoon grated nutmeg, dash of MSG, $^1/_2$ cup milk, 1 egg (beaten).

Fry the green pepper, celery and mushrooms in a little butter. Combine minced beef, oats, MSG, salt and pepper, egg and milk. Pat the meat mixture on to a board or waxed paper to form a rectangle about 8″ x 15″. Spread over the fried green peppers, celery and mushrooms. Starting with the short end, roll up as you would a Swiss roll. Place roll with seam side down in a well-greased loaf pan. Bake in a preheated oven for about 1 hour at 180° C (350° F). Allow to stand for five minutes before slicing. Serve with a rich brown gravy. A rasher of streaky bacon may be placed underneath and on top of the roll when it is baked.

Note: Use oatmeal to extend tastily all minced meats.

Silwood's Steak and Kidney Pudding

With an Old-fashioned Suet Crust

For the Filling: 1 onion, 500 g (1 lb) beef steak, 2 sheep's kidneys, 125 g (4 oz) buttered mushrooms (tinned), 1 dessertspoon flour, a little fat, salt, pepper, 300 ml ($^1/_2$ pint) stock (made with beef cubes).

For the Suet Crust: 250 g (8 oz) self-raising flour, a pinch of salt, 125 g (4 oz) shredded suet, cold water to mix.

To Make the Filling: Peel and slice the onion. Trim and cut the steak into large cubes. Skin, core and cut the kidneys into four. Melt the fat in a sauce-pan and toss the sliced onion and meat in the hot fat until lightly browned. Add the mushrooms. Remove the pan from the heat and stir in the flour, seasoning and liquid. Bring to the boil, cover and simmer gently for about $1^1/_4$ hours.

To Make the Suet Crust: Sift the flour and salt into a mixing bowl and stir in the shredded suet. Add sufficient cold water to make a stiff dough, then knead on a floured board until it is quite smooth. Keep $^1/_8$ of the dough for pudding top. Roll out remaining dough and use it to line a 900 ml ($1^1/_2$-pint) greased pudding basin. Press the lining gently but firmly round the basin edges.

Pour in the prepared and slightly cooled meat mixture. If the stewed meat is too hot it will spoil the suet crust. Roll out the remaining dough into a round to fit exactly the top of the pudding basin. Damp the edges well with cold water, then lift the top carefully on to the lined and filled basin. Press the edges firmly, to make sure that the pudding is sealed all the way round.

Cover the top of the pudding with a double round of greaseproof paper and tie securely with string below the rim of the basin, then tie on a damp pudding cloth. Steam the pudding for $1^1/_2$–2 hours. Remove the pudding cloth and paper when the pudding is cooked.

To Serve: Tie a clean napkin round the basin and place on a serving platter. Sprinkle the top of the pudding, if liked, with chopped parsley.

Bobotie (1)

> 500 g (1 lb) mince or tinned corned beef, 450 ml ($^3/_4$ pint) milk, 1 thick slice of bread, 2 onions (minced), 2 tablespoons butter, 1 tablespoon curry powder, $^1/_2$ teaspoon salt, $^1/_2$ teaspoon sugar, 2 tablespoons lemon juice, 2 eggs.

Soak bread in cold milk. If using corned beef chop finely. Fry mince and onion in butter until lightly browned. Stir in lemon juice, salt and curry powder. Stir well (do not allow to burn) and cook gently for 10 minutes. Place this mixture into mixing bowl. Squeeze out all milk from soaked bread. Add bread to mince mixture. Add 1 beaten egg and beat well with fork. Pour this into well buttered pie-dish. Beat remaining egg and add milk from soaked bread ($^3/_4$ cup). Season with pepper and salt and pour over meat mixture. Scatter small dabs of butter on top. Place pie-dish in another pan containing water and bake in moderate oven at 180° C–200°C (350° F–400° F) for 40 minutes until pie is set and a light brown on top. Serve with rice or vegetables.

Bobotie (2)

Traditional Malay

Bobotie can be prepared from fresh mince or left-over cold meat. The former is, of course, more appetizing. Here is another typical recipe for bobotie:

> 2 onions (finely sliced), 1 apple (diced), 2 tablespoons butter, 1 kg (2 lb) minced cooked meat, 2 slices bread, soaked and squeezed out, 2 tablespoons curry powder, 2 tablespoons sugar, 2 eggs, 2 tablespoons vinegar, 2 teaspoons salt, $^1/_4$ teaspoon pepper, $^1/_4$ cup raisins, 12 almonds (optional), 6 bay or lemon leaves, 1 cup milk, 1 teaspoon tumeric (optional).

Fry the onion and apple in the butter and mix with the meat, bread, curry, sugar, 1 egg, vinegar, salt, pepper and raisins. Blanch and remove skins of the almonds, cut almonds into quarters and add. Mix well. Place in a greased baking dish. Roll the lemon leaves and insert them well into the mixture in an upright position. Bay leaves are not rolled. Bake in a moderate oven for 30 to 45 minutes. Beat the second egg with the milk and pour it over the bobotie about 10 minutes before it is removed from the oven. Serve with rice and chutney. When raw mince is used the cooking period is about $1^1/_4$ hours.

Bobotie (3)

1 kg (2 lb) topside mince, $^1/_2$ teaspoon cloves, $^1/_2$ teaspoon onion salt, 2 teaspoons salt, 1 teaspoon turmeric, 1 tablespoon vinegar, 1 tablespoon water, 2 eggs (beaten), 2 onions (sliced), $^1/_2$ teaspoon nutmeg, 1 teaspoon ginger, 1 dessertspoon apricot jam or chutney, 2 teaspoons curry powder, 1 tablespoon sugar, lemon leaves.

Brown onions in butter, add mince and 1 cup water and simmer for 10 minutes, stirring constantly and browning on all sides. Mix all dry ingredients with vinegar and water and add to mince. Simmer further for 10 minutes over low heat, stirring constantly. Pour into an ovenproof dish. Cover with beaten eggs and arrange lemon leaves on top. Bake at 180° C (350° F) for 30 minutes. Serve with yellow rice and raisins. 8 Servings.

Water-Flower Bredie

Waterblommetjiebredie: (See Colour Plate)

In springtime when the *wateruintjies* are flowering like snowflakes on the Cape vleis, the Coloured people gather them for this delectable mutton dish. At Silwood Kitchen we have served this 'traditional' to overseas guests with congratulatory results.

Although the dish is usually made with mutton many people prefer a vegetarian version. For this merely omit the meat. The cooking may be done on top of the stove or in the oven. Slow cooking is essential or the flowers will break.

2 kg (4 lb) thick fat rib of mutton, 2 medium-sized onions (cut finely), 2 little bundles wateruintjies (picked when fully opened, washed, with stems cut off), 1 small bundle sorrel (chopped finely), 1 cup boiling water, 1 cup dry white wine (if no sorrel is available), 1 large potato (cut into fine slices), salt and a pinch of sugar, pepper to taste.
pinch of sugar, pepper to taste.

Sprinkle the meat with salt, sugar and pepper, then brown it. Remove from the saucepan. Sauté the onions till golden brown in the same fat. Add water-blommetjies, and place the potatoes on top. Simmer all gently until tender but not broken. Serve with steamed rice.

Bredie Using Wateruintjies

Dr Louis Leipoldt's way

The late Dr Louis Leipoldt was fond of *wateruintjiesbredie*. He prepared it as follows: Use 2 to 3 soup plates full of wateruintjies for 1 kg (2 lb) of mutton. Pick the flowers off the stems and remove the hard bits underneath; soak them in salt water overnight. Before adding to the seasoned meat give them a quick boil up in water, then strain.

Tomato Bredie

1 kg (2 lb) ribs of mutton, large onion (sliced), 8 tomatoes (skinned), 1 teaspoon sugar, pepper, salt, small piece of red chilli (optional), potatoes.

Cut up the ribs of mutton in pieces large enough for individual servings. Melt some soft fat or dripping in a saucepan. Add the onion and stir till a golden yellow. Add the meat. Cover the saucepan and let the meat and onion cook slowly for about an hour. Slice tomatoes and add to the meat, add seasoning and sugar. A small piece of red chilli may be added if desired. Stew for another hour. Add peeled potatoes cut in quarters. Continue cooking till the potatoes are soft. Serve with boiled rice.

Pumpkin Bredie
With Mutton

1 .5 kg (3 lb) lamb or mutton (cut into cubes), 4 medium-sized onions (cut into rings), 6 cups raw pumpkin cubes, 2 capsicums (sweet red peppers), finely chopped after pips and stem have been removed, a dash of cinnamon and powdered nutmeg, salt and pepper to taste, Knorr Aromat, a pinch of sugar, a blade of mace, 1 bay leaf, 1 tablespoon margarine or dripping.

Into a shallow, heavy, iron or steel pot, put the shortening and meat and fry until richly brown, pouring off and keeping any gravy that forms. Remove the meat and keep hot. Now lightly fry the onions and the chopped red peppers (adding more fat if necessary) until just beginning to get tender. Return the meat and gravy to the pot, plus the pumpkin cubes, salt, pepper, Knorr Aromat, sugar and spices. Cover tightly and continue cooking over a low heat. If the pumpkin is of the very dry kind, add a little meat stock, but in most cases, the gravy formed by the cooking pumpkin will be sufficient. If there is too much liquid when the meat is tender, leave off the lid, and the liquid will evaporate until the right consistency – that of thick gravy – is attained. Be careful not to burn, though. Serve with yellow raisin rice, or new potatoes.

Chopped cabbage or sliced beans may be used instead of pumpkin, but these must be par-boiled before adding them to the meat and gravy in the pot. (If green beans or cabbage are used instead of pumpkin, leave out the cinnamon.)

Stuffed Suckling Pig

The sucking pig should not be over 6 weeks old. It is cooked with these (uncooked) ingredients:

2 chicken livers, 185 g (6 oz) mushrooms, 2 onions, 1 tablespoon of meat glaze, 2 raw eggs, parsley, dill, marjoram, tarragon, 185 g (6 oz) butter, MSG and pepper.

All ingredients should be chopped and the butter and glaze melted. Mix all in a basin, stuff the pig and sew it up. Roast for $1^1/_2$ hours or till well done, basting frequently. Serve with a purée of potatoes mixed with cream and a gravy made from the bastings, and an apple in its mouth.

(For more information write to Director, Silwood Kitchen, Rosebank, C.P.)

Pork Hot Pot

Better Today Than Ever Before

> 500 g (1 lb) pork fillet or tenderloin, approximately $^1/_2$ cup stock, 500 g (1 lb) potatoes, 250 g ($^1/_2$ lb) onions, 125 g (4 oz) prunes, salt, pepper, MSG, a pinch of sugar, 30 g (1 oz) packet of sage and onion stuffing, 1 medium cooking apple, 2 tablespoons oil, 1 tablespoon butter.

Soak the prunes overnight. Cut the pork meat into 25 mm (inch)-size pieces. Peel and slice the potatoes and onions, cut the soaked prunes in half and remove the stones. While browning the meat in the oil and butter make the stuffing and peel and slice the apple. Put the potatoes, pork, onions and prunes in layers in a casserole, seasoning each layer with salt, pepper, MSG and sugar. Add about 150 ml ($^1/_4$ pint) of stock or enough to come two-thirds of the way up. Cover and cook slowly for $1^1/_2$ hours, or until the meat and potatoes are tender. Spread the stuffing over the top of the hot pot and arrange the apple slices on that. Place at the top of a moderately hot oven and cook until the apples are brown. Serve from the hot pot.

No accompaniments are necessary, except perhaps a green vegetable, such as cabbage, brussel sprouts or green beans.

Kop en Pootjies

In Pressure Cooker

This traditional South African recipe, once cooked on the old coal stoves for hours on end, may be done in 45 minutes using a pressure cooker at 7 .5 kg (15 lb) pressure.

> Pig's head and trotters (cleaned and prepared by butcher), 3 peeled and sliced onions, $^1/_2$ cup breadcrumbs, 1 tablespoon butter, grated nutmeg, salt, pepper, 1 cup tomato pulp (optional).

Soak the head and trotters in salt and water brine for about 15 minutes. Cut the head in half (cutting away the nose bones and bones above the eyes if the butcher has not done this). Divide the trotters and cut into 3 or 4 pieces. Remove the gland between the toes, then wash head and trotters in several waters. Put all the meat into the cooker with the onions, adding just sufficient water to cover. Cook 40 minutes – when bones should easily slip from the toe-part of the trotters. Reduce pressure, open cooker and add breadcrumbs, butter, nutmeg, salt, pepper and tomato pulp and simmer gently for 15 minutes. Remove the large pieces of head bone before serving. Thicken gravy if too thin.

Family Budget Bean Stew

Not Only Filling but Tasty too

> 340 g (11 oz) red or brown beans, 1 tablespoon olive oil, 1 large onion, 1 large carrot, 2–3 cloves garlic, 2 red peppers seeded and shredded, 1 teaspoon tomato purée, about 1 litre (4 cups) stock or water with beef cube, 250 g ($^1/_2$ lb) pre-cooked salt pork or ham pieces, 2 frankfurter sausages blanched and thickly sliced, 250 g ($^1/_2$ lb) good ripe tomatoes, peeled and halved, salt, pepper, chopped parsley.

Cook beans well beforehand. Sauté onion, carrot, garlic and peppers for 7–10 minutes. Add beans, cook for further 10 minutes, stirring several times to prevent burning, add tomato purée and stock. Cover the saucepan and bring to boil slowly. Add pork or ham, simmer slowly for 1¹/₂ hours, add sausages and tomatoes. Cook slowly for 25 minutes more. Place in a pre-heated chafing dish. Serve piping hot, dusted with chopped parsley. (Add stock from time to time, if bean stew thickens too much during cooking.)

How to Smoke Hams

To two large hams or three small ones, take 2¹/₂ kg (5 lb) common salt and ¹/₄ kg (250 g) of brown sugar. Mix together and rub well into the hams. Let them lie for a week, turning them every day while you rub more of the salt sugar mixture into them. On the seventh day rub a mixture of 120 g (4 oz) salt-petre and a handful of common salt into the hams. Allow them to lie a fort-night longer. Then hang up high in a chimney to smoke.

Ham Stuffed with Fruits

Hams in our old days were often stuffed with fruits after the bone had been removed. A favourite stuffing was apricots, raw, mixed with breadcrumbs to absorb the juice, seasoned with salt and pepper. When the stuffing had been pressed into the hole the whole ham was wrapped in its flour and water paste and baked. When it was cold the crust was cracked off and the ham was glazed and studded with cloves or the apricot kernels.

Today's Festive Glazed Ham

With Mandarin Oranges

1 large tinned ham, 1 can mandarin oranges, 1 tablespoon maizena, ¹/₂ cup orange marmalade, 1 tablespoon angostura bitters, 1 teaspoon dry mustard, 1 tablespoon cider vinegar, ¹/₂ teaspoon ground cloves, whole cloves.

Remove the ham from the can and put on a rack in a shallow roasting pan. Drain the oranges and mix the juice slowly into the maizena in a saucepan. Add the orange marmalade, angostura bitters, mustard, vinegar and ground cloves. Cook over low heat, stirring constantly, until thickened. Score top of ham in a diamond pattern with a sharp knife. Bake in a preheated moderate oven 180° C (350° F) for one hour. At this time brush the ham with angostura glaze, both top and sides. Bake for an additional 30 minutes, brushing glaze over ham several times. Remove from oven and decorate the top with man-darin orange sections.

Ham Smothered with Sweet Potato

1 slice of smoked ham, cut into sizes for serving, 3 cups raw, sliced sweet potatoes, 1 tablespoon butter or ham drippings, 1 cup hot water, sugar.

Brown the ham slightly on both sides and arrange it to cover the bottom of a baking dish. Spread the sliced sweet potatoes over the ham. Sprinkle with sugar. Add the hot water and extra fat. Cover the dish and bake slowly until the ham is tender. Baste the potatoes occasionally with the gravy. Brown the top well.

Today's Variation: This is one of our favourite supper dishes. Use thickly sliced (tinned) ham. Drench in pineapple juice. Spread slices of already cooked (steamed) sweet potato over the ham. Sprinkle with sugar or dab over a little warmed honey; dust with breadcrumbs and slightly brown top under the grill. Serve with sweetcorn and/or green peas.

Veal

Not a Tradition

While hundreds of ways of preparing veal appear in all old European cook books, veal has but a small place in older cook books here and certainly cannot be classed under a traditional heading. The reason is that in addition to this young meat not keeping – it taints very quickly – our old economic farming factors are to be considered. Yet because of its popularity and the availability of veal today here is our demonstration method for the true Wiener Schnitzel.

Wiener Schnitzel

Although a schnitzel is cut from a leg of veal, it is not a veal steak. For a true schnitzel the meat should not be cut straight across the grain, but on a slant, half with and half against the grain, and the slices should be about 3 mm ($^1/_8''$) to 6 mm ($^1/_4''$) thick. After the slices are trimmed, they should be pounded gently, with a flat mallet, from the centre and outwards until they are very thin – sufficiently thin to cook through in one minute. The purpose of pounding is to partially break down, but not crush, the fibres of the meat. The pounded slices are marinated in lemon juice for an hour and should be turned frequently while they are marinating. Snip the outer edges with scissors, to prevent curling when put into the hot fat. Ingredients required are:

> 1 kg (2 lb) veal steak, 12 mm ($^1/_2''$) thick, 2 eggs (seasoned), 4 tablespoons seasoned flour, salt, pepper, sugar, lemon juice and Aromat or Zeal, fine dry crumbs (seasoned), butter for frying.

Marinate the veal in lemon juice for 30 minutes. Cut into serving pieces and dry with a kitchen towel. Sprinkle with salt, pepper and Aromat. Dip into the seasoned flour, then into the seasoned egg (well beaten), coat with seasoned breadcrumbs. Fry in hot fat (butter and oil) until brown on both sides. Serve with a garnishing of lemon wedges.

For a variation, add grated cheese to the crumbs, or for a special occasion mince finely 125 g ($^1/_4$ lb) ham; allow to dry like breadcrumbs, then mix with the breadcrumbs and coat the veal as described above. (In Austria lard is used for frying.)

Veal and Ham Rolls

Today's Budget Treat

> 250 g ($^1/_2$ lb) pie veal, 1 onion, 1 clove garlic, 60 g (2 oz) oatmeal, seasoning and paprika, 1 tablespoon parsley, beaten egg, 30 g (1 oz) corn-flakes, 60 g (2 oz) butter, 2 slices ham, 60 g (2 oz) cheese. Serves 4.

Trim veal, removing fat. Cut up and mince. Mix with grated onion, crushed garlic, oatmeal, seasoning, paprika, and chopped parsley. Mix in egg. Divide the mixture into 4 portions. Place on greased paper. Cover with second sheet of greased paper. Roll out to 6 mm (¼″) thick. Coat escallops in cornflake crumbs. Fry in butter for 8–10 minutes. Halve slices of ham, roll up. Place one on top of each escallop and then sprinkle with grated cheese. Place under hot grill for a few minutes to soften and brown the cheese. Serve on a bed of spaghetti, garnished with sliced tomato and parsley.

Goat's Meat

Goat's meat is eaten by urban Africans as well as their relations in the home-lands and it is stocked by butchers in the Bantu settlements. The skin from a young goat is used for threading tribal beads – being durable and pliable.

Although our Bantu people either simply stew or roast goat's meat over a fire according to the age of the meat the more sophisticated recipes for cooking goat came from the East, including curried goats meat. Most lamb recipes can be applied to kid and for a full-grown goat treat as mutton. Treat goat chops like mutton chops but remove the bone which is longer than that of a sheep. Break the bone off close to the head bone and cut it away leaving the roll of fat; fold the fat up and fit it into the inner side of the chop, fastening with a skewer. Then cook as a mutton chop.

Sweet and Sour Goat

For Any Tough Meat

This recipe, brought by Malays from the East, can be used for any coarse tough meat. Simmer the meat until tender in plenty of water with salt and pepper. Pour off the gravy into a large saucepan then add fresh herbs such as rosemary, thyme, sage and parsley or greens as available, such as spinach. Boil up and add a tablespoon of finely shredded fat, and then spices such as cloves, powdered cinnamon, mace and a piece or two of root ginger. Now place in a clean flour bag a selection of raisins, currants, dates and prunes. Tie the top of the bag and place it in the pot with the herbs and spice to simmer in water to which you should add a tablespoon of grape juice and vinegar. When the fruit is plump and cooked within the bag, add the already cooked meat to the broth and continue to simmer for five minutes.

To serve: Cut the meat into neat pieces on a heated dish placing the hot fruit from the bag on top. Strain the broth, add a little brown sugar to taste and dry sherry or cider and boil until syrupy. Pour this over the meat and fruit. Garnish with fresh orange segments and almonds.

Marinated Goat's Meat

Old Karoo Recipe

1 leg of goat, 250 g (½ lb) sheep-tail (or spek) salted, 2 cups vinegar, 1 dessertspoon salt, ½ teaspoon pepper, 4 cloves, cooking fat, boiling stock, Aromat, a pinch of sugar.

Lard the leg of goat with strips of tail fat. Stick cloves into the meat. Place it in an earthenware dish and pour seasoned vinegar over. Leave in a cool place for 1 to 2 days, turning occasionally. Dry the meat and brown it in hot fat in a heavy iron saucepan. Add boiling stock (25 mm – 1″ – deep). Cover and allow to simmer until the meat is tender. Replenish the liquid with boiling water or stock when necessary. Long simmering is necessary.

Crown Roast of Lamb Karoo

Order a minimum of 2 best end necks of lamb. Ensure that the main (chine) bone has been chopped through between each cutlet, that all skin has been removed and that surplus fat has been trimmed away.

To Prepare and Tie: Assemble a trussing needle, fine string, strong scissors and a small, sharp, preferably pointed knife. Trim away skin and flesh scraps between the bone tips on each neck. Cut bone tips with scissors into neat points so that a stuffed olive or cherry can be impaled on each after roasting. Place the two pieces of meat, eye of cutlet end on board with the inside of each piece outwards. Thread one end of string into needle and push it through the last cutlet of one piece 2 .5 cm (1″) above the eye, from the outside to centre. Bring it back by poking the needle from the inside through in precisely the same place on the other piece. Now tie the string firmly so that the two pieces are held together and snip off ends neatly. Bend the two pieces of neck until they meet – thus forming a hollow circle with the pared bone tips curving outwards and upwards. Re-thread the needle and repeat the tying together as explained for the previous stage, but in this case leaving plenty of string before knotting. Then take two ends of string right round the 'waist' of the two pieces crossing them at opposite sides and bring them back to where they started. Tie off securely. Push a closed fist down in the centre and force the tied meat into a very neat circle. (Your butcher will do this for you if you give him some advance notice.)

Stuffing

500 g (1 lb) beef sausage, 250 g (¹/₂ lb) pork or veal sausage, Stuffed olives, gherkins, pecan nuts, pickled walnuts, fingers of ham or tongue, salt, pepper and a pinch of sugar, Knorr Aromat.

Garnish: Cutlet frills, glacé cherries or stuffed olives, mint or parsley.

Fill crown ²/₃ full of well-mixed sausage meats. Put olives or gherkins, pecan nuts or pickled walnuts, at intervals into stuffing. Push ham or tongue through at suitable points, staggering them so that a pattern is formed when the crown is sliced. Put the crown in a roasting pan, brush all over with melted fat and cover top with a circle of doubled aluminium foil or a small potato to prevent tips blackening during cooking time. Roast on the centre shelf at 180° C (350° F) allowing 25–30 minutes per 500 g (1 lb).

Garnish with mint or parsley, press a cutlet frill, glacé cherry or stuffed olive over each bone tip and serve with drained canned pear halves filled with mint jelly. For clarity refer to colour plate at beginning of this book.

*   *   *

Traditional Tourists' Tip

For atmosphere and food evocative of the best of our Cape past, pay a visit to David Rawdon's *Lanzerac,* as well as his *Matjiesfontein,* Cape.

Venison

Traditional Luxury Everywhere

Recipes for cooking venison abound in all the old British cook books as well as those of this country. In Victorian times big hunts were arranged for the Queen's birthday. Warnings are given that although the meat should be hung well and be a little high when cooked it should not be kept so long as to begin to decay. In this country all meats, for the White population anyway (some tribal peoples are not affected by decomposing meat), are treated differently to those of Europe.

Our own big game hunters favour the following for venison: eland, springbok, duiker, steenbok, klipspringer, sable antelope, redbok and oribi.

The hunter would cook the head of the buck in the campfire overnight, eat it the next day then take the carcase home for his wife and her servants to deal with. Favourites were young venison steaks cut from the legs, basted well with fat and red wine then grilled wrapped in a thick bacon rind. (The salt from the rind reddens the meat, but no matter.) The haunch is considered the best joint. The neck is treated as chops.

Old tough meat was braised. After boning we are advised to 'beat one way then t'other' with long flat strokes. Marinate covered well in wine or vinegar and oil, then brown in fat, lay in a covered casserole and simmer until tender.' It was served with quince jelly. A traditional rule is never to have thick brown gravy with venison. The gravy should be clear and bright made from the meat juices and red wine of the marinade.

Roast Springbok or Duiker

Hang the saddle or leg for 3 days. After the buck has been skinned, a thin white fleece remains, which must be removed before larding the venison. Take a piece of fat bacon and cut it into strips, and lard the venison with a larding needle or pointed knife. Lay the larded meat in a basin (never metal) and pour on 600 ml (1 pint) red wine, 300 ml ($^1/_2$ pint) vinegar, adding 2 bay leaves, 6 peppercorns, 4 cloves and 2 onions, sliced. Leave in this mixture for 3 days, turning the meat twice a day. Wipe well and place in a flat roasting pot with a little water. Cook gently and then add salt, and a good piece of butter and some fat. Keep turning and basting the meat until it is a good brown colour.

Half an hour before serving, pour over the strained wine and all in which the venison has been soaking and to which has been added a spoonful of flour and 2 spoonfuls of quince or kei-apple jelly. Stir the gravy well. Serve with quince, kei-apple or amatingula jelly. (For the latter see *Index*.)

Venison Pie

2 kg (4 lb) shoulder of venison, 1 tablespoon apricot jam or chutney.

Marinate venison for 2–3 days in the following mixture:

1 cup red wine (medium), 1 teaspoon ginger, $^1/_2$ teaspoon cloves, 1 teaspoon thyme, 4 teaspoons salt, $^1/_2$ cup vinegar, 2 teaspoons coriander, 2 teaspoons nutmeg, 1 teaspoon onion salt, 1 tablespoon Worcestershire sauce.

Turn the venison every day.

Before cooking you can spread meat with apricot jam or chutney. Slightly dilute this mixture with water, place in casserole together with venison and cook slowly, adding water when necessary until meat comes off the bone. Remove bones and mash meat. At this stage add about $^1/_4$ kg ($^1/_2$ lb) of finely chopped pork fat (spek), return to stove and cook about 30 minutes, stirring constantly. Thicken mixture slightly. About 30 minutes before serving pour venison into an ovenproof dish and cover with pastry. Place in a hot oven – about 200° C (400° F) – and leave until golden brown (20–30 minutes). Serve with apple jelly.

Pastry

2 cups flour, $^1/_2$ bottle soda water, 250 g (8 oz) margarine.

Rub margarine into flour. To bind: squirt soda water on to mixture (one third to one half bottle). Leave in fridge to cool until required.

Simple Pot Roast Venison

Leg of venison, bacon rashers as required, 1 bottle red wine (Chianti type), 2 cloves of garlic crushed, small tin tomato paste with 2 teaspoon sugar, a pinch of oregano.

Wrap streaky bacon rashers completely round the leg. Place in roasting pan, pour over wine that has been mixed with the tomato paste and sugar and herb. Cover and simmer until meat is tender, adding a little boiling stock or water with bouillon cubes when necessary, and turning frequently. Serve with its own gravy, slightly thickened and with fluffy mashed potatoes and a red currant, quince or clear sorrel jelly.

Mock Roast Venison

Using Scotch Fillet

1 .5 kg (3 lb) scotch fillet steak, 250 g ($^1/_2$ lb) bacon, 1 glass red wine, oil, salt, pepper, MSG, a pinch of sugar, 2 garlic cloves, foil.

Marinate the meat in wine for 3 or 4 hours (24 hours if it actually is venison). Take the meat out of the liquid and dry it. Make small cuts in it at intervals with a sharp knife, filling each one with a little roll of bacon. Season well, and rub it with oil. Sprinkle all over with flour, place into foil (shiny side up), and the halved garlic cloves around it. Wrap it up and bake in a medium oven at 150° C (300° F) for 1 hour. Open the tin foil, remove the garlic cloves and brown the roast under the grill, turning it often, and basting it. You can add a piece of fat or a few tablespoons of salad oil. When ready, thicken the gravy adding browning to taste.

Marinaded Venison and Other Meats

Prepare 48 Hours in Advance

This marinade may be used for beef, venison, and lamb. (If using topside cut in cubes and leave a little fat in it.) To the meat add basic mixture:

1 sliced carrot, 1 sliced onion, 1 clove garlic (cut very small), 2 bay leaves, 3 or 4 cloves, ground pepper (black), *no salt,* red wine or dry white wine – to almost cover.

If using venison only add this basic mixture. (For other meats the following may be added as well: lemon leaves, 1 teaspoon fennel, 1 pinch thyme, 1 teaspoon tarragon vinegar, peel of about $^1/_2$ orange.)

First pour a little oil on top to prevent meat going black. When required, drain from marinade and brown meat in mixture of oil and butter. Add 2 tomatoes, peeled and cut into small pieces, 1 level tablespoon flour, salt, to taste. Now add marinade again, put in an iron pot and the longer and slower it cooks the better. About 4 hours at 130° C–150° C (250° F–300° F).

Pickle For Beef or Tongue

Dissolve 1 .5 kg (3 lb) salt, 15 g ($^1/_2$ oz) saltpetre, 180 g (6 oz) brown sugar in 4 .5 litres (one gallon) water, boil for half an hour. Skim and cool. Put the meat or tongue into this, turning every day or two. Allow eight to fourteen days for beef, according to the size of the joint, and four to six weeks for ox tongues.

Biltong

An exclusively South African product going back to Bushman times is our biltong – the same word in English and Afrikaans, although in old books *tassel* or *tasseltjies* is used (from the Portuguese *tassalho*); but strictly speaking *tasseltjies* means preserved meats.

The main difference between our biltong and the dried meats of other countries is that from beginning to end biltong is raw and not ground, as distinct from the American Indian's pemmican. Since the Vietnam war its popularity with the G.I.'s has led to production in U.S.A. under the name of 'jerky'. According to an old issue of the Wall Street Journal, an army aviator downed in enemy controlled jungle claimed that he and a companion survived for a week on two packages of jerky and a roll of lemon candy before they were rescued, and the report concludes. 'One American dealer when he was shown the new jerky remarked: "Now we're not even selling the horse here, we're selling the saddle".'

Talking of saddles reminds us of soldiers during the Boer War who would shoot game, eat as much as they could, then cut the rest into long strips which they placed between the flaps of the saddles and saddle cloth for the heat of the horse's body to cure it.*

While in other countries dried meat is roasted our biltong is spoilt by cooking. Biltong may be made from the leg and thigh of almost any animal, from lion to goat, ostrich to ox and, even fish biltong is made. The art lies in the cutting and the curing and although this is a specialised business (more fully dealt with in our *Cookery in Southern Africa Traditional and Today*) here we give a short recipe, indicating the ingredients.

How to Make Biltong

Biltong consists of long pieces of meat (cut with the grain) which are salted and then dried. Venison is considered the best biltong but beef, ostrich and many kinds of meat are used for this typically South African dried meat.

---

* The saddle method of curing meat was known to marauding Huns – nomadic horesmen – from ancient times.

The following quantities are for 25 kg (50 lb) of meat.

2 kg (4 lb) No 1 coarse salt, 125–250 g ($^1/_4$–$^1/_2$ lb) sugar, 15 g ($^1/_2$ oz) packet bicarbonate of soda, 2 tablespoons coriander seed, 1 tablespoon pepper.

Mix all the spices and salt together, and rub half the quantity into the meat. Place the biltong in layers in a bath or similar container, sprinkling the remainder of the spices and salt over the top. Leave for 24 hours, with a heavy weight to press it down. Before it is hung up, every piece of biltong must be rolled on a table, in order to give it a good shape. Hang in a cool, clean ventilated place until dry.

Ideas for Using Biltong

Biltong, either bought in strips by the kilo or in packets conveniently grated is specially good for topping savouries in sandwiches combined with egg or mixed with cottage cheese. For example, a log of cottage cheese made savoury with grated Cheddar, chopped olives, horseradish, cream and a dash of garlic can be covered with grated biltong for a pleasing "log" effect.

Rabbits

Rabbit was a favourite meal in Britain, but often denied the poor by the severe poaching laws. Even as late as 1815 a law was passed punishing with seven years deportation any man found in possession of a net for catching rabbits. No wonder the 1820 settlers anticipated freedom in leaving for a land which, if not flowing with milk and honey, had abundant game free for the shooting – if not rabbits. The Dutch East India Company had banned importation of them to the mainland and directed they be 'tried out' on Robben Island – where they were exterminated by the snakes.

In this country wild rabbits, like hares, have suffered a certain ill reputation for worms, but now that they are sold by butchers from farmed sources and fed with balanced rations (like chickens), rabbit, reinstated, appears on the best menus. The flesh of the rabbit is so similar to that of chicken most recipes for chicken dishes apply.

Rabbit Pie

English Settlers' Recipe

Put into the bottom of a baking-dish a few slices of ham or beef; cut the rabbit into as many bits as you like; season each bit with salt, pepper, pounded spices, etc. Put them in a dish as close as possible, add a glassful of broth if you have any; if not, a wine-glassful of water and a drop of white wine. Cover this dish quite close with a good crust, beat an egg and brush it over the paste. Bake in a hot oven for an hour and a half, when the pie will be ready for serving. Whether hot or cold, this dish is excellent. Remember that if the rabbit pie is to be eaten cold it must be much more highly seasoned than when made to be eaten hot.

The Fine Art of Currying Favour

The Cape Malays who came from Batavia and who were our first South African cooks naturally gave their masters the same spicy Javanese dishes they had enjoyed as servants of the Dutch East India Company in the East. Then about 200 years later came the forefathers of our Indians to Natal recruited for the sugar industry – who today practically run the food business. No wonder South Africans favour curries and spicy foods!

Our Indian Chef's Rules

If you are a purist you'll cook curry in either mustard oil or ghee (clarified butter obtainable from Indian shops). If not then use butter combined with sunflower or olive oil or any good fat. Select young vegetables and chop them as finely as possible. Never allow them to discolour while frying.

Do not further thicken your curries by adding white sauce or flour – unless indicated by the recipe – rather allow the curry to simmer slowly to thicken itself by evaporation. If the resultant curry must be thickened, add cream, evaporated milk or *malai* – the thick skin that forms after milk has been boiled; grated coconut is also excellent for thickening.

Do not stir the curry too much; rather shake the pot. If it must be stirred, use a wooden spoon, previously dipped in boiling water.

Curries should be tasted before serving and the seasoning corrected. Fresh lemon juice added to curry enhances its flavour.

Chicken, fish, hard-boiled eggs, prawns or root vegetables all make good curries; if they are cooked they should only be re-heated in the sauce. If the chicken, meat or vegetables are cooked entirely in the sauce add a little extra stock at the beginning, as it will evaporate during the cooking. Always remember to cook a curry *slowly*.

(For the full curry story see Lesley Faull's *Rice Recipes and Curries.*)

Indian or Cape Malay Curry

With Mutton or Beef as You Wish

2 onions (sliced), 1 garlic (chopped), 1 kg (2 lb) mutton (diced), 1 brinjal (chopped up), 3 green chillies (chopped)*, 250 g (¹/₂ lb) dried apricots (soaked), 1 teaspoon turmeric*, 1 teaspoon coriander*, ¹/₂ piece crushed raw ginger*, 1 green pepper (chopped), stick cinnamon, 1 tin tomato purée, 1 teaspoon ground jeeru*, 1 teaspoon barishep*, about 2 teaspoons vinegar or to taste, chutney (to taste), 1 cup buttermilk or yoghurt, 1 cup apricot jam (or to taste), MSG (Zeal), pinch of sugar.

Fry the onions and garlic, add the meat (mutton or beef as you decide), and when browned add all the other ingredients except the jam, chutney and buttermilk or yoghurt. Simmer slowly until tender, then add the buttermilk or yoghurt, chutney and jam.
Serve with accompaniments.

Vegetarians' Variation: Add diced nut meats to the sauce 15 minutes before serving.

---

* All these ingredients are obtainable at Indian Shops.

Basic Curry Sauce

45 g (1½ oz) margarine or dripping, 1 small onion, finely chopped, ½ cooking apple, finely chopped, 2–4 tablespoons Madras curry powder (to suit your own taste), ½ level teaspoon salt, 1 teaspoon curry paste (optional), 250 ml (1 pint) stock (or coconut infusion), 1 bay leaf, 1 clove garlic, ½ level teaspoon caraway seeds (pounded together). To thicken: 1 level tablespoon cornflour – blended with 4 tablespoons stock or water. Additional flavourings (optional): 1 teaspoon black treacle or molasses, 1 tablespoon chopped mango chutney, few sultanas, lemon juice.

Melt the fat in a heavy pan. Add onion and apple and cook gently 5 to 6 minutes. Stir in curry powder, pounded garlic mixture, salt and curry paste. Stir in the stock – which has been thickened with cornflour – smoothly. Bring to boil. Cover closely and simmer about 30 minutes.

Home-Made Curry Powder

As Made by Indian Chefs

Home-made curry powder – fairly strong – can be made as follows:
Roast for a few minutes and then grind together:

60 g (2 oz) cumin seed, 185 g (6 oz) coriander seed, 15 g (½ oz) fenugreek, 30 g (1oz) black peppercorns.
To these add the following, ground but not roasted:
30 g (1 oz) cloves, 60 g (2 oz) cinnamon, 30 g (1 oz) cardamon, 30 g (1 oz) mace, 60 g (2 oz) red chillies. (All are obtainable from Asiatic stores.)

Leave the chilli seeds in if you want to raise the palate roofs of all who partake of your curries – otherwise remove them. Sieve all the ground ingredients together and store in an air-tight jar.

Serve These with Your Curry

Yellow rice with raisins; home-made fruit chutney or commercial chutney; grated coconut (this is delicious if sautéed carefully in a little butter until crisp); chopped nuts; pawpaw balls sprinkled with lemon juice; pineapple with tamarind; seedless raisins; chopped green peppers; diced cucumber, mixed with salt and sour cream; diced banana, sprinkled with lemon juice; relishes of all descriptions (obtainable in large supermarkets); preserved ginger; French-fried shoestring potatoes; French-fried onion rings; hard-cooked eggs, whites chopped, yolks sieved; watermelon or green tomato sweet pickle; quince preserve; glazed dried apricots or peaches; crisply-fried bacon, chopped; sousboontjies, using butter beans (see *Index*); cottage cheese; mixed diced tomato and onion; avocado segments; Bombay Duck (obtainable in any Indian shop); roti (Indian bread); popadams (fry in hot oil until crisp, and crumble over curry); spiced currants; crunchy peanut butter, fried (stir briskly over low heat in well-oiled pan); yoghurt.

Spiced Currants

Simmer the following for an hour, then seal when cold:

500 g (1 lb) currants, ½ teaspoon cinnamon, ½ cup malt vinegar, 1 cup brown sugar, ½ teaspoon cloves.

Ostrich Eggs

Don't let's miss what Lady Anne Barnard had to say about some that she 'exported'. The following is an excerpt from a letter she sent to Henry Dundas (British Secretary for War and Treasurer of the Navy):

I also send you a box of ostrich eggs, the freshest I could obtain. I am told, by boiling them well, and packing them with bran they often keep to reach Holland good. There are six eggs, one of them being emptied by me to make some cakes and try if it was good. Nothing could be more capital.

To Cook an Ostrich Egg

One ostrich egg is equivalent to 22–24 hen's eggs. Being so much richer it is imperative that the contents of the egg once opened should be used within 24 hours. One beaten white and yolk is about $4^1/_2$ standard cups; The eggs need more beating than hen's eggs.

To Boil: Cover a fresh ostrich egg completely with cold water and bring to the boil. Simmer for one hour. Serve with yolk mashed with a little butter and the mashed white around on a platter. Garnish with tomato slices or tomato sauce. Some people like it with Worcestershire sauce. The mashing of yolk and the white separately can be done with a potato masher, adding salt and pepper to taste.

Seal's meat, duikers, penguins and penguin eggs were included on the menu of our first South Africans.

Curried Penguin Eggs

Now Seldom Available

Hard-cook the eggs by placing in cold water with a dash of vinegar and bring to boil. Boil for $1/_2$ hour, then shell them while still hot; if you wait till they are quite cold, the jellied white is apt to get tough. Take out the yolks and mash them with some lemon juice, salt and pepper. Replace in white, and set aside in a warm place. Warm your curry powder – a teaspoonful for every two eggs is enough – in a pan, stirring it constantly, and when it is nicely warmed add some coconut milk* and stir until it gets hot. In another pan fry a finely chopped onion, a minced chilli, a pinch of ground ginger. Add your curry mixture to this, and let it simmer. Finally, whisk into it a few tablespoons yoghurt or cream. When it thickens, put the eggs in and let them get well saturated with the sauce. Dish up with rice and a sweet chutney.

Salt of Our Earth

Salt, the most important preservative from earliest times was for centuries a costly ingredient, in some cases costing as much or more than the meat or fish to be salted. Fortunately for our early South Africans Van Riebeeck discovered saltpans one month after his arrival. As he recorded in his journal May, 1652: *We shall not require salt, having found . . . a beautiful salt-pan near the wreck of the Haarlem* – presumably along the Diep River a few miles from the future Fort. The threatened fouling of the saltpans caused such concern that an edict was soon issued: *No one may dig salt without a permit from the Company's overseer.*

* Steep grated coconut in boiling water for 20 minutes, then strain.

Samoosas

The perfect samoosa is one that is a perfect triangle, and has no corner left gaping, not even the tiniest gap. If any point has an open niche, then oil will seep through when samoosas are being fried, making them soggy and unattractive. Keep filled samoosas in a cool place and fry when required.

Fry samoosas in deep oil over medium heat, turning them over a few times so that they are evenly browned. Remove from the pan when a lovely buff cream shade. Drain in colander. Serve with lemons and chutneys.

The following detailed instructions for making samoosas are by courtesy of Z. Mayat, editor of *Indian Delights* (produced by the Women's Cultural Group, Durban). All the ingredients are available at Indian stores.

Khima . . . Master Mince Recipe

For Filling Samoosas

500 g (1 lb) mutton or chicken mince, 2 medium-sized onions (chopped very fine and thin), 2 teaspoons pounded green chillies, 1 teaspoon salt, 1 teaspoon ginger/garlic, $^1/_2$ teapoon gharum masala, 1 tablespoon ghee, 1 small bunch dhunia leaves (washed and cut fine), 2 tablespoons green shallot (washed and cut fine), 2 tablespoons green mint (washed and cut fine) – optional.

Wash and drain the mince. Braise in frying pan with salt, ginger/garlic and green chillies. When dry, add onions and braise just enough till moisture is evaporated. Add ghee*. Khima should now be fine and dry like breadcrumbs. Cool khima and add the cut-up greens (well washed and drained dry) and gharum masala.

Indian Pastry

Indian pastry is basically made of flour with very little shortening. It is then divided into equal portions and each portion rolled out to paper-thin rotis. Each roti is then brushed well with melted ghee, sprinkled with flour and piled one on top of the other, leaving only underside of the bottom roti and top side of roti ungreased. If large amounts of dough are handled at a time, then as many rotis are rolled out as the recipe calls for, but the average housewife who works with as little as 1 or 2 cups of flour at a time, will welcome this short-cut method introduced here.

Assuming 1 cup of flour is handled, divide the dough into 4 sections. Roll each out to paper thinness. Brush each roti well with melted ghee and sprinkle flour (or a little flour braised in ghee) over. Pile rotis on top of one another. Now roll the pile of discs into one large roll with smooth swift strokes. Trim off sides to form a square.

Put roti on hot ungreased griddle iron plate. Toss and turn lightly several times on both sides in order to separate layers. Deftness in turning will ensure that it does not become freckled. As soon as the layers appear loose, remove from griddle and move aside.

* Clarified unsalted butter.

When slightly cool, trim and cut into 5 cm (2″) wide strips by 25 cm (10″) long. Separate layers and fill samoosas. To fold, first fold along CD, then CE along EF, so that D falls on F. Now hold strip of pastry between thumb (Point B) and forefinger of left hand and fill pocket with 2 teaspoons of mince. Now fold EF over pocket so that G falls at point C. Then fold FG over pocket so that H falls on E, then HG again over pocket and so on till the strip is used up. Paste final length down, with a mixture of flour and water.

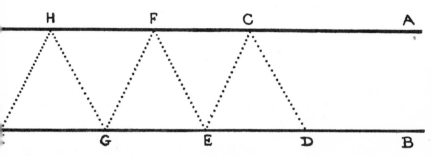

We suggest you practise on a strip of paper first, to get the knack of folding samoosas neatly. The dotted lines on the illustration will indicate how to use the strip for folding.

Cold Water Paste Recipe

1 cup flour, 2 teaspoons ghee (unsalted butter), $1/2$ teaspoon baking powder, $1/8$ teaspoon salt, a few drops of lemon juice, cold water.

Rub the ghee into dry ingredients. Make into a fairly stiff dough with the lemon juice and cold water. Roll out into 4 portions and prepare as above.

Hot Water Paste Recipe

1 teaspoon ghee (unsalted butter), pinch of salt, sufficient flour to form a firm dough, $1/2$ teaspoon baking powder, $1/4$ cup milk, $1/4$ cup water.

Bring the water and milk to the boil. Remove from the stove and pour into a mixing bowl. Add to the hot water and milk, the salt, baking powder and ghee. Add as much flour as is needed to form a stiff dough. Divide into 4 portions and prepare as above. (This makes 16 layers.)

POTTAGE – PORRIDGES – GRUELS

As the old adage suggests, *to keep one's breath to cool one's porridge,* a porridge is usually served hot, but not always, as is proved by the Swiss muesli. It is not only served at breakfast but often makes a meal for any time of day, and every country has its own form of porridge for serving sometime. Quite often it can be confused with a cereal soup, for it is usually based on some cereal.

Most famous of all our porridges is traditional Putu made from mealie meal and today inseparable from boerewors at the braai.

Putu – Traditional

Afrikaans: Poetoe

Lumps of this special steamed mealie meal porridge are served to mop up the gravy with grilled boerewors.

2 cups white mealie meal (unsifted, if possible), 4 cups water, 1 rounded teaspoon salt.

Boil the above together for $1^1/_2$ hours, in the following way: Bring water to the boil with the salt. Pour mealie meal in a pyramid in the middle of the pot. Reduce heat to low and allow to simmer for 45 minutes, then open up the pyramid with a wooden spoon, flick it, and allow the mixture to simmer 10 minutes more, vigorously stirring any remaining moisture into the cooked mixture until it is smooth and thick and holds it shape. Now gently pour $^1/_2$ cup cold water down the sides of the saucepan. Stir in, cover and allow to steam another $^1/_2$ hour on a low heat.

Putu

A Farmwife Explains

Putu is more nourishing if one or two cups of milk are poured over it when cooked and then put into the oven to bake for an hour or more; and eaten with sour milk instead of sweet milk.

A nice change is to make a pudding with 'putu' as you would a rice pudding, and another change is to bake the mealie meal in the oven to a very light brown colour before you make the porridge (not 'putu'). The natives drink a quantity of what they call 'magau'.

Magao Marewu

Our Domestics Love It

Cook a rather thin porridge for an hour or two. No salt. Take off the fire, stir until lukewarm (if you do not stir it forms lumps which spoils it), add 1 or 2 tablespoons of yeast, any yeast will do. In 24 hours it will be ready. Farmers' wives often use 2 or 3 cups of this 'risen' porridge to make bread.

Krummelpap

Crumbly Porridge . . . for Two

Add $^1/_2$ teaspoon salt to $^1/_2$ cup water and boil. Add 1 cup maize meal and boil slowly for 15 minutes. Stir with fork till mixture becomes crumbly. Simmer for 20–30 minutes till well cooked.

CAPE COOKERY WITH KELP

All health enthusiasts are acquainted with the nutritional properties of edible seaweed. The revival of interest in this subject and the prospects of kelp farming to ease the plight of the world's hungry millions convinces us we must give some space to Cape authorities on the subject here; but more information will be found in our *Cookery in Southern Africa Traditional and Today* (in libraries). A natural seaweed jelly is obtainable now in packets but there is no reason why we should not revert to that happy pastime of collecting *Suhria vittata* again and enlivening our food with delicious home-made jellies.

Jellies from Seaweed

The Malays introduced edible seaweed into our Cape cooking. In a letter sent in 1962 to Miss Woodgate of the Cape Natural History Club by Mrs W. de Villiers of Sir Lowry's Pass, Mrs de Villiers tells of how a milk pudding made out of this seaweed was evolved by her mother. In her childhood days the liberated Malay slaves who remained in the service of her grand-parents made a sort of seaweed blancmange which they called *gooma*. They boiled it and strained it and ate it with sugar and milk like one eats porridge.

Further information in a leaflet in the possession of the Secretary of the Cape Natural History Club tells us that the seaweed is collected at low tide from the stems of the sea bamboo *(Ecklonia buccinalis)* – whose hollow dried stalks were used as fish horns (before the tin horns superceded them) to herald the approach of the Cape fish carts.

If the sea bamboos have been long exposed to the sun, the seaweed *(Suhria vittata)* may be bleached white instead of its natural red colour, and may be hard and brittle. But red or white, fresh or dry, hard or soft, it is equally good for jelly-making. The sea flavour is more pronounced in jelly made from the fresh seaweed.

According to the leaflet referred to above, the following recipe was evolved and used for years by the first Club Steward, Miss Giftie Biggs.

Take a handful of the seaweed (i.e. about the size of a tennis ball when squeezed together), wash well, and boil to a pulp in 3 to 4 pints of water.

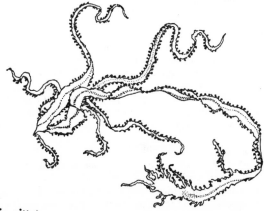

Suhria vittata.

When brought to the boil, leave lid off for about a quarter of an hour for the 'seaweedy' fumes to steam off. Strain through cloth and add sugar, lemon or orange juice, brandy or sherry, all to taste. (One cupful of sugar to a pint is generally enough.) Pour into small containers to set. A large mould is not advisable unless it is all to be eaten at one meal, as the jelly is liable to liquefy partially if cut into and left.

Additional flavouring can be imparted by adding cloves, cinnamon, and several pieces of lemon peel to the boiling seaweed, but these should be put into a muslin bag and removed after boiling for about a quarter of an hour.

Seaweed Jelly

V. M. FitzRoy's Method

In her *Eat and be Merry* V. M. FitzRoy gives instructions for making seaweed jelly as follows:

The seaweed collected from the sea bamboos has to be dried in the sun and shaken free of sand. Wash well in several waters, tie in a muslin bag and boil in plenty of water. Flavour with cloves, wine, lemon and sugar, and when the liquor is gelatinous pour it at once into glasses. It sets quickly and it is difficult to get it to dissolve again afterwards. The seaweed can be kept in its bag and used several more times, each time with a little extra flavouring. The sea taste is strongest with the first boiling and fades with each successive one. This jelly is delicious and nourishing, with a high iodine content.

There was a definite belief in its therapeutic properties in the old days, for Mrs FitzRoy tells of how a child regained health after a serious illness when fed on the jelly. The future may prove those instincts of our ancestors right. As has been noticed before in this book, the pendulum of the past swings steadily fore and aft, for and against; items once treasured, now discarded, can come into their own again.

Tschin-Tschou

Jelly made from Suhria vittata

This recipe, more or less in the words of a fisherman at Hout Bay, is given in Hilda Gerber's *Traditional Cookery of the Cape Malays:*

Soak the pink seaweed, which you find growing on the large sea trumpets in Hout Bay, for 24 hours in cold water. Renew the water several times. Throw away the soak-water and use the cleanly washed seaweed just like you would use gelatine. (Only the seaweed is much nicer than gelatine.) Boil up the seaweed with freshwater and scum it from time to time. When it is clean add any kind of flavouring you like. Either take lemon essence, vanilla essence or any other flavouring and some sugar and then a few drops of colouring to make it look nice. Some people use rose-water and a little crushed cardamon seed; others use milk instead of water. This seaweed is just like gelatine and even if you make it too thick it is still nice because it then becomes a sweet like Turkish Delight. It never gets leathery, however much you take. The old man added with a superior chuckle: 'The only reason that white people don't use this good thing is that they don't know it. We Malays know what's good to eat.'

Sweet Afterthoughts.

Puddings & Accompaniments

Cape Town 1768

It is recorded that in 1768 Mrs Neethling ran an excellent boarding house for 10 officers in Cape Town . . . *who spent their time in a comfortable parlour where a table stood always laden with peaches, melons, apricots, raisins, pears, cheese, fresh butter, wine, pipes and tobacco. Tea and coffee with bread and butter were served at 8 a.m.; fish and game in plenty at noon, and supper at 8 p.m. partook of the same nature.* Inclusive charge was 2/- a day. Prices were doubled a few years later when the French fleet arrived.

Golden Honey Fluff

This was served at the Cape Town Gourmet Society dinner in honour of Silwood Kitchen's first patron, M. André Simon, C.B.E., M.M., on 12th March, 1965.

> 1 packet orange jelly, $1^1/_4$ cups boiling water, $^1/_2$ cup chilled unsweetened evaporated milk, $^1/_2$ cup honey, 1 dessertspoon of sugar, juice of a large lemon.

Dissolve the jelly crystals in boiling water. Add honey and lemon juice, and let this begin to thicken. Beat until thick and frothy. Whip chilled milk until thick and frothy and fold into jelly. Pour into a wetted ring mould to set in fridge. Unmould and serve with apricots or peaches and ice-cream *or* whipped cream.

Orange Ginger Jelly

Heat 1 cup orange juice, heat 1 cup ginger ale, add 1 dessertspoon sugar. Melt an orange jelly and sugar with above and beat well. Add 1 cup ginger ale, beat well and set in a wetted mould. Chill and turn out later. Serve with custard or cream.

Lemon Gin Seaweed Jelly

From Silwood Kitchen

Cook a small jelly size packet of natural seaweed according to the packet instructions, but use one cup less water and in its place add half a cup of gin and half a cup of fresh lemon juice and a drop of lemon oil. Then add brown sugar or honey to taste, and strain into a mould. Allow to set.

Fruit Fools

In the 18th century people were partial to 'fools' for dessert: *a kind of clouted creame called a fool or a trifle, stewed fruit mixed with milk cream or custard,* are two definitions. Today we can make all kinds of fools from our fruits, working on the foolproof principle of folding puréed fruit into the cream or, like this from Silwood Kitchen, using gelatine to set the fool.

Guava Fool

10 guavas, 5 tablespoons sugar, 1 dessertspoon gelatine, 1 cup custard, $^1/_2$ cup cream.

Boil the guavas until very soft. Mash them, and strain them through a sieve. Add the sugar and cook until quite thick. Dissolve the gelatine in 1 tablespoon of water over hot water; when dissolved, add it to the guavas. Add the custard and lastly the cream. Pour into individual cups or into one big serving dish. Leave in the refrigerator until needed.

Banana Fool

2 cups banana pulp, 3 or 4 egg yolks (well-beaten), 2 tablespoons brandy, rum or maraschino, $^1/_2$ cup thick cream (whipped), 2 egg whites (beaten), 2 tablespoons of castor or icing sugar, $^1/_8$ teaspoon nutmeg (grated). Serves 6.

Mash the bananas with a fork to fill 2 cups and whip the pulp – using an electric blender if you have one, otherwise an egg beater. Beat the egg yolks until thick with a pinch of salt, add banana pulp and brandy. Beat again well. Pour this mixture into sherbet glasses and chill. Before serving, whip the cream and whip the egg whites with sugar; fold into each other and top each glass with this fluffy egg white cream mixture – which is less rich than whipped cream – although of course this can be used if liked. Sprinkle a little nutmeg over the top of each serving or chopped nuts, as desired.

Silwood's Peach Crumb

With Dried Peaches

500 g (1 lb) dried peaches, $^1/_2$ cup sugar, lemon rind, 125 g ($^1/_4$ lb) butter, $^1/_2$ cup castor sugar, 1 cup self-raising flour *or* 1 cup cake flour and 1 teaspoon baking powder, $^1/_2$ cup coconut.

Cover the fruit with cold water and add sugar and lemon rind. Simmer until the fruit is soft. Place it in an ovenware baking dish. Cream the butter and castor sugar. Sift in the flour and add the coconut. Rub in with the finger-tips until the mixture resembles coarse crumbs. Sprinkle this over the fruit mixture and bake at 190° C (375° F).

Cape Angel's food

Dissolve a packet lemon jelly and a packet granadilla (or orange) jelly in 3 cups hot water and add a cup of strained granadilla juice. When almost set whip the jelly and fold in 1 cup whipped cream. Set in fridge. Some people leave the granadilla pips in, for crunchiness.

Pears on Vineleaves

Those with vineleaves in their gardens can try this 17th century recipe for pears – evidently those rather tasteless hard ones.

Put a layer of vine leaves in an earthen pot then a layer of peeled halved pears, then leaves and pears again, with one or two cloves. Fill up the pot with cider (we suggest alternatively a sweet wine and water, honey, or sugar with a fruit syrup from canned fruit.) Cover the pears and place in a low oven overnight at 140° C (275° F) until pears are tender. Serve cold on a vine leaf with whipped cream and sugar.

The Tempting Apple

Who was the first to discover the love affair between buttered bread and apples? Our Irish cousins still delight us with a baked apple on a round of bread crisply fried both sides in butter. (Home-made bread *and* butter, of course.) But all old cookbooks include some apple-bread idea. Here are some of them:

Buttered Apple

With Bread Cubes

Chop and cube peeled apples, then drop into a bowl of castor sugar. Melt just enough butter in a heavy frypan to fry the sugared apple pieces, stir and turn until the pieces are a golden sticky brown. Place on a hot serving dish while you fry some white or brown bread cubes using a little more butter. Turn these and stir until they mop up the caramel left from the apple. When crisp toss apple and fried bread together and serve instantly with castor sugar strewn over and a little hot cider or dry sherry if liked.

Great Aunt-Anne's Apple Cake

750 g (1¹/₂ lb) cooking apples, 85g (3 oz) unsalted butter, 85g (3 oz) castor sugar, grated rind and juice of 1 lemon, 2 tablespoons water, 125 g (4 oz) fresh white breadcrumbs, 125 ml (¹/₄ pint) thick cream, 1 tablespoon any red seedless jam.

Peel, core and slice the apples into a large saucepan. Add 30 g (1 oz) of the butter and 30 g (1 oz) of the sugar, the lemon rind and juice and the water. Cook gently until the apples are soft. Cool. Melt the remaining butter in a shallow pan with the remaining sugar. Add the breadcrumbs and fry gently until browned. Cool. Arrange alternating layers of apple and crumbs in a glass serving dish. Whip the cream until thick but not stiff and spread it over the top. Decorate with spoonsful of jam or pieces of preserved fruits.

Crumb Top Apple Pie

6 to 8 cooking apples (Granny Smiths), ²/₃ cup granulated sugar, ¹/₂ teaspoon nutmeg, ¹/₂ teaspoon cinnamon, 2 tablespoons cold water.

Peel and core apples and slice into a deep oblong pan. We use a loaf pan. Sprinkle over the apples the sugar, nutmeg, cinnamon, cold water.

In another bowl mix:

90 g (3 oz) butter, $^1/_2$ cup brown sugar, 1 cup sifted flour and a pinch of salt.

Mix this with finger tips until it is the consistency of coarse meal. Sprinkle this over the apples. Bake in a slow oven 50 to 60 minutes. This may be served either hot or cold and with vanilla ice cream or whipped cream.

Apple Sponge

With Dried Apple Rings

$1^1/_2$ cups self-raising flour, 60 g (2 oz) butter, 1 large egg, a pinch of salt, $1^1/_2$ cups milk, 2 tablespoons white sugar, 250 g ($^1/_2$ lb) dried apple rings, 4 cloves and 2 pieces of stick cinnamon or lemon peel, 2 tablespoons brown sugar.

Cover apple rings well with cold water and leave to soak overnight. Add brown sugar, cloves and cinnamon or lemon peel and simmer gently until all the water has been absorbed.

Sift the flour and salt together and rub in the butter. Whisk egg and sugar together and add milk. Gradually stir egg and milk mixture into the flour mixture. Place the cooked apple rings in a greased heat-proof glass dish. Pour the dough mixture over the apples while they are still warm. Bake for 35 minutes at 190° C (375° F).

Silwood's Toffee Apples

For All Children Through the Ages

Toffee apples derived from medieval fairs – even before sugar came into general use. Windfall apples were dipped in a toffee of honey and beeswax. Today we make ours at Silwood Kitchen as follows:

375 g (12 oz) golden brown sugar, 185 g (6 oz) golden syrup, 30 g (1 oz) butter, $^1/_2$ cup water, 1 teaspoon lemon juice (or vinegar), 1 dozen small red apples.

Wash, dry and polish apples well. Remove stalks and force a wooden skewer into the stalk end of each. Put all the other ingredients into a thick saucepan and heat gently until the sugar is fully dissolved. Bring to the boil and cook briskly without stirring to 150° C (300° F), when a drop tested in cold water will snap cleanly. Dip the apples into the toffee, twisting to coat completely, and then immediately into a bowl of cold water. Leave to set on a greased tray.

Melk Tert

600 ml (1 pint) milk, 2 tablespoons butter, 4 tablespoons sugar, 2 eggs, 4 tablespoons flour *or* 1¹/₂ tablespoons Maizena (cornflour), stick of cinnamon, *or* 1 teaspoon naartjie peel.

Scald the milk in a double boiler with the cinnamon or peel. Mix the sugar and flour or maizena, and add the hot milk, slowly, stirring well. Return the mixture to the double boiler, and cook for 15 minutes with the lid on. Remove from the stove and stir in the butter. When cool, add the eggs, one at a time, mixing well. Line a tart plate with flaky pastry, and pour in the mixture. Bake in a hot oven at 230° C (450° F) for 20 minutes, with good heat at the lower part of the oven. Reduce the heat for the last ten minutes. Powdered cinnamon and sugar may be sprinkled over just before serving.

Van der Hum Tart

A Silwood Kitchen Speciality

4 tablespoons butter, ³/₄ cup sugar, 1 cup shelled chopped Brazil nuts, 1 cup coconut.

Cream the butter and sugar. Mix the nuts and coconut well, and then rub them with the fingers into the butter mixture. Press into a pie plate, building up the sides. Bake for 12–15 minutes at 190° C (375° F), until slightly brown. Cool.

Filling: 6 egg yolks, 1 cup castor sugar, 1 tablespoon gelatine, ¹/₂ cup cold water, 2 cups cream, ¹/₂ cup Van der Hum, cherries to decorate. Serves 8.

Whisk the egg yolks very well. Add the sugar, and beat until light. Soak the gelatine in cold water, then melt it *over* hot water. Add the egg mixture and beat well. Whip the cream, fold into the egg mixture, add the liqueur, cool and add to the baked shell. Decorate with whipped cream and cherries.

Dutch Potato Tart

For Those with Almond Trees

In our pursuit of traditional cookery we feel we must not leave out the almond; it was always almonds almonds all the way, sweet and bitter, like life itself – more sweet to bitter, in most recipes, happily.

Hildagonda Duckitt quotes this recipe for almond tart, using mashed potatoes and almond for the filling.

Line a pie-dish with puff paste. Fill with the following:

125 g (¹/₄ lb) potatoes (boiled and mashed), 6 well-beaten eggs, 100 sweet almonds, 24 bitter almonds, blanched and pounded and mixed with rose water and 125 g (¹/₄ lb) sugar. Bake as usual.

Old Fashioned Treacle Tart

Fill pastry shell with ³/₄ cup warmed golden syrup mixed with 1 cup bread-crumbs, juice and rind of a lemon and a pinch of salt. Bake.

Pumpkin Pie

Pumpkin pie is an old English (Cornish) pie that went over with the Pilgrim Fathers on the *Mayflower* and came to South Africa via the old and the new worlds. Here is the old English recipe.

After steaming the pumpkin until tender, put it through a sieve and to 600 ml (1 pint) of pulp add the following:

2 eggs (well beaten), $^1/_2$ cup milk, $^1/_2$ cup treacle or molasses (obtainable from some supermarkets or chemists), 125 g ($^1/_4$ lb) brown sugar, 2 tablespoons butter, $^1/_2$ teaspoon of ginger and cinnamon, $^1/_2$ grated nutmeg, pinch of salt, 250 g ($^1/_2$ lb) shortcrust pastry.

Line a pie plate with shortcrust pastry. Mix all the above ingredients and pour the mixture into the pie shell, baking for 30–40 minutes in a moderate oven. When cold, decorate with whipped cream.

Old-Fashioned Sour Cream Raisin Pie

Lesley's Recipe for Now

1 cup sour cream (if sour cream is not available, condensed milk, un-diluted, gets almost as good results), $^1/_2$ cup seeded raisins (ground after scalding and draining), $^1/_2$ teaspoon cinnamon, $^1/_4$ teaspoon cloves, 1 cup sugar, 3 beaten egg yolks, 1 egg white.

Line the pie-dish with your unbaked pie crust dough and fill with the above custard. Bake in a hot oven for 10 minutes, then reduce heat so that custard bakes slowly. After the pie is baked, beat the remaining 2 egg whites until thick, add 2 tablespoons of sugar and beat until the mixture holds to points. Spread on hot pie, return to slow oven and brown meringue.

Tansy Pudding

Really a Rich Custard

Very old cook books frequently refer to tansy puddings, where the juice of tansy (leaves of the plant *Tanacetum vulgare*) was taken at Easter – being associated with the bitter herbs of the Passover. The following is an adaptation of an ancient recipe:

Take 125 g ($^1/_4$ lb) of almonds and pound well. Place in a pan with a gill of the syrup of roses, the crumb of a large bread roll, $^1/_2$ glass brandy, 2 tablespoons tansy juice, 90 g (3 oz) fresh butter, and a few slices of citron. Pour over 3 cups of hot milk or cream and, when cool, add the juice of a lemon and 8 eggs, beaten. Grate a little nutmeg over, and bake to set in a slow oven, or steam as for custard.

Custard in a Pumpkin

An Old Malay Dish

This unusual dish made by descendants of Malays from the Far East will please vegetarians who are looking out for something 'we've never had before', as the custard can be converted to a savoury.

Select a firm ripe pumpkin 1 kg–1.5 kg (2–3 lb), one that will stand squarely with the stem end up. Cut off this stem end to form a lid. Now scoop out the seeds and some of the flesh. Make some coconut milk by pouring boiling water over freshly grated coconut (or shredded coconut from an Indian store or failing that desiccated coconut from the supermarket) and leave to steep for 20 minutes. Mix the water and shredded coconut well with a spoon and press through a sieve or cloth. The liquid only is used – this is the coconut milk. Beat 4 large eggs with 2 tablespoons sugar, adding the coconut milk gradually. Pour this mixture into the partially hollowed out pumpkin, replace the stem top lid of the pumpkin and steam it; this may be done by placing it on a rack in a saucepan with a little hot water in the bottom. When the pumpkin is soft and the custard is set, the dish is ready to serve. Small squashes may be filled with a custard in the same way. Serve with honey as a sweet, or convert to a savoury with grated cheese, omitting the sugar.

Orange Candied Sweet Potatoes

With Marshmallow Topping

> 1 cup orange juice, $^1/_2$ teaspoon grated orange rind, 1 cup water, 6 medium sized sweet potatoes, 1 cup sugar, $^1/_4$ cup butter, $^1/_2$ teaspoon salt.

Peel and slice uncooked potatoes in 6 mm ($^1/_4''$) slices and arrange in a buttered baking dish. Make a syrup of the ingredients and pour over the potatoes. Cover and bake in a moderate oven until tender. Baste occasionally. Remove the lid the last ten minutes and allow to brown. A layer of marshmallows may be added and browned just before removing from the oven.

The Marmalade Roll Mother Made

As Made at Silwood Kitchen

> 2 cups flour, pinch of salt, 2 teaspoons baking powder, 125 g (4 oz) shredded suet, 6 tablespoons marmalade, 2 tablespoons castor sugar.

Set the oven at 190° C (375° F). Grease a large baking sheet. Sift the flour, salt, sugar and baking powder into a bowl. Stir in the suet and enough cold water to form a soft dough. Roll out on a lightly floured board into an oblong. Spread with marmalade, leaving a 24 mm (1″) edge all round. Turn long edges in 3 mm ($^1/_8''$), moisten. Roll up from one of the short edges. Seal edges. Put roll on to a baking sheet. Cook in the centre of the oven for 35–40 minutes or until golden. Serve very hot with custard.

Christmas Puddings

When the 1820 British settlers came to this country they did their best to perpetuate their idea of a traditional Christmas. But it didn't always work to the satisfaction of their means or their digestion. One of the settlers, John Sheddon Dobie, who wrote in his diary much about the early days of hunger and frustration, recorded that he celebrated his first Christmas Day with 'boiled beef, pudding, raisins and almonds', but 'couldn't sleep at night what with the heat and the pudding!'

Mr Dobie was not the first, neither is he the last, to discover that hot Christmas pudding cannot be traditionalised here with our high summer temperatures, and even if you wait until the cool of the evening to eat it, it can lie 'heavy on the stomach'. For this reason most South Africans prefer a cold Christmas pudding served with ice cream to complement the roast and that's why we give here, in addition to our hot puddings, cold puddings – now rapidly becoming a true South African tradition.

How to Steam the Pudding

Puddings must be steamed in boiling water that comes half-way up the sides for as long as the recipe states. Add more boiling water as it is required, but never allow the water to come up too high or your pudding will be ruined. If you haven't a grid to fit the bottom of the saucepan it is a good idea to allow your pudding bowl to stand on a folded dishcloth or thickly folded newspapers in the pot.

To Flame the Pudding

Warm the brandy *before* you try to light it. Either stand the brandy in a pan of hot water for a minute or use a warm silver spoon or punch ladle to pour it over the pudding. Set alight with a match – never use a cigarette lighter. Don't try to re-flame the brandy when the first flames have died.

Our Hot Christmas Pudding

The quantities given yield two 20 cm (8'') diameter puddings plus one 12 .5 cm (5'') bowl.

350 g ($^3/_4$ lb) sultanas, 350 g ($^3/_4$ lb) cherries, 350 g ($^3/_4$ lb) seeded raisins, 750 g (1$^1/_2$ lb) currants, $^3/_4$ cup mixed peel (chopped fine), $^3/_4$ cup shredded almonds, 1$^1/_2$ cups grated carrots, $^3/_4$ measuring cup butter (very soft but not liquid), 1$^1/_2$ cups stale breadcrumbs, 1$^1/_2$ cups milk, 1$^1/_2$ cups brown sugar, juice and rind of 2 lemons, 9 eggs (beaten), 3 cups flour, $^3/_4$ teaspoon salt, 1 teaspoon nutmeg, 1$^1/_2$ teaspoons allspice, 1$^1/_2$ teaspoons cinnamon, $^1/_4$ cup and an extra dash Oude Meester brandy.

Mix fruit, carrots, butter, nuts, crumbs, milk, sugar, juice and rind of lemons. Cover and allow to stand overnight.

Add beaten eggs, flour sifted with salt and spices. Add the brandy last. Put in bowls adding usual charms – which have previously been cleaned and boiled. Cover with wax paper and linen. Boil seven hours. Boil a further two hours before serving.

Old Fashioned Brandy Sauce

Made from Soft Custard

In a double boiler, place 2 cups of milk, 4 beaten egg yolks and either 2 tablespoons sugar and 1 tablespoon grated lemon rind *or* 2 tablespoons of citrus sugar,* and $^1/_4$ pint of brandy. Cook, stirring well until thick and creamy. Keep hot and serve with the pudding.

*See sugars by referring to *Index*

Brandy Butter

To Serve with all Christmas Puddings

250 g ($^1/_2$ lb) butter, 250 g ($^1/_2$ lb) castor sugar, $^3/_4$ tumbler of brandy, approximately (or to taste), chopped cashew nuts, cherries, chopped angelica for decoration.

Cream the butter and sugar very well (until snow-white and fluffy). Add the brandy gradually, little by little, mixing well until the result satisfies your individual requirements. Stir in the chopped nuts and cherries, keeping sufficient for decoration. Pile up in a glass dish, top with nuts, cherries and angelica, and put in the refrigerator until required.

This sauce is best made the day before it is to be used. Left-overs can be kept indefinitely if stored in an air-tight container and placed in the refrigerator.

Hard Sauce Stars

125 g ($^1/_4$ lb) butter, 125 g ($^1/_4$ lb) castor sugar, 125 g ($^1/_4$ lb), sifted icing sugar, 2 tablespoons rum or liqueur brandy.

Beat the butter to a cream, then beat in the sugar. Beat in liquid, a little at a time, until flavoured to taste. Chill slightly in the refrigerator, then pipe large stars onto wax paper laid over a baking sheet or in the bottom of an ice-making tray, and leave in the freezing compartment of the refrigerator for about 12 hours. The stars will come free of the wax paper quite easily. Top with a piece of cherry and angelica. Serve chilled with hot Christmas Plum Pudding and cream.

Our Famous Frozen Pudding

With an Ice Cream Foundation

A large aluminium or metal steamer or copper mould, 185 g (6 oz) raisins, 125 g (4 oz) prunes, 125 g (4 oz) mixed glace fruits (pineapple, pears, ginger, apricots), 185 g (6 oz) sultanas, 185 g (6 oz) currants, 60 g (2 oz) chopped mixed peel, $^1/_2$ cup Oude Meester van der Hum liqueur, rum or fruit syrup, 90 g (3 oz) blanched almonds (chopped and toasted), 60 g (2 oz) crushed peanut brittle, 60 g (2 oz) dark chocolate (grated), 60 g (2 oz) maraschino or glace cherries (quartered), $^1/_2$ cup cream (whipped), 2 litres Walls vanilla ice cream, a pinch salt.

Chop the raisins, prunes and glacé fruits and mix with the sultanas, currants and mixed peel. Sprinkle with rum and allow to stand for several hours or overnight. Then lightly and quickly fold all the ingredients into the slightly softened ice cream. Pack the mixture into the mould. Cover the top with aluminium foil and freeze overnight. To unmould the ice cream: quickly dip the mould in and out of warm water. Turn on to a serving dish. Decorate with holly, whipped cream, fruits and nuts as desired. Serves 8–10.

An Easy Jellied Pudding

1 packet orange jelly, 1 packet lemon jelly, $1^1/_2$ cups seeded raisins, $^2/_3$ cup sultanas, $^1/_3$ cup mixed peel, 2 apples (peeled and finely grated), $^1/_4$ cup chopped almonds, $^1/_3$ cup brandy or orange juice, 4 cups hot water, 12 ginger biscuits.

Dissolve jellies in hot water, and leave till thickened but not set. Steam the raisins, sultanas and mixed peel in the top of a double-boiler for about 1 hour. Soften the biscuits in brandy or orange juice. Blanch the almonds and chop very fine. Stir the biscuis into the thickened jelly, add the steamed fruit, nuts and apples. Pour the mixture into a quart mould and chill till firm. Decorate with cream and holly.

Festive Mincemeat

Mincemeat improves with keeping because as the fruit is uncooked it needs time to swell and absorb the flavour of the spices and spirits used in the making.

250 g (8 oz) of the following: currants, stoned raisins (chopped), sultanas, dates (chopped), mixed peel (chopped), prepared shredded suet and brown sugar, 150 ml ($^1/_4$ pint) Oude Meester brandy *or* Ricardo white rum, 150 ml ($^1/_4$ pint) sherry, 2 large cooking apples (grated), 125 g (4 oz) blanched almonds (finely chopped), finely grated rind and juice of two lemons (*or* lemon and orange), good pinch of ground ginger, good pinch of cinnamon.

To make mincemeat combine all the ingredients.

Mince Pies

Take one cup of sour cream, one cup soft butter, 2 cups flour, teaspoon castor sugar and a pinch of salt. Mix all ingredients together but avoid kneading. Roll dough out thinly for pie bases and tops. Insert mincemeat. Bake at 180° C (350° F) and when baked, sprinkle pies with icing or castor sugar.

Brown Bread Pudding

A Nourishing Austerity Pudding

250 g ($^1/_2$ lb) brown breadcrumbs, 250 g ($^1/_2$ lb) shredded suet, 250 g ($^1/_2$ lb) currants, sugar and nutmeg to taste, 4 eggs, 2 teaspoons cream, a little brandy if liked, a little milk.

Mix together the breadcrumbs, currants, suet, sugar and nutmeg. Add the beaten eggs, the cream, and brandy, if liked. Add milk if necessary. The mixture should be fairly stiff. Put it into a well-buttered basin, cover with a piece of greased paper and stand the basin in a saucepan with boiling water halfway up. Steam for 3 hours. Serve with golden syrup separately.

Pumpkin Fritters

4 cups cooked mashed pumpkin, 1 tablespoon sugar, 2 tablespoons flour, salt to taste, 2 eggs, 2 teaspoons baking powder.

Mix the pumpkin, sugar and flour together. Add the well-beaten egg yolks, then fold in the stiffly-beaten whites. Lastly add the baking powder and salt. Drop dessertspoonfuls of the batter into hot cooking oil and brown on both sides. Sprinkle the fritters with cinnamon and sugar and serve hot with lemon wedges.

Fruit and Rice Fritters

Using Left-over Rice and Soft Fruits

Mix any left-over rice with any soft fruit (raw pears, plums or cooked, drained stewed fruit of any kind). Sweeten to taste. Bind the fruit and rice mixture with sufficient beaten egg and drop into hot fat or oil, about a tablespoon at a time. Serve with sugar, cinnamon, syrup or sweet sauce.

Souskluitjies

Traditional Sweet Dumplings

3 tablespoons Maizena, 2 tablespoons flour, 3 tablespoons custard powder, $^1/_4$ teaspoon salt, 4 cups milk, 2 eggs (separated), 1 teaspoon vanilla essence, $^1/_2$ cup melted butter, cinnamon sugar. (For latter see *Index*.)

Combine the maizena, flour, custard powder and salt and mix to a paste with a little of the cold milk. Bring the rest of the milk to the boil, stir in the flour mixture slowly. Stir continuously until it thickens, taking care that it does not burn. Beat the whites and yolks of the eggs separately. Add the yolks to the custard mixture and mix well. Remove from heat and fold in the stiffly beaten whites. Add the essence. Put the mixture, a tablespoonful at a time, into a serving dish, pouring half teaspoon melted butter and one teaspoon cinnamon sugar over each dumpling. Pour over the rest of the butter. Serve hot.

N.B. A mixture of $^1/_4$ cup melted butter and $^1/_4$ cup boiling water may be used instead of $^1/_2$ cup melted butter.

Stampkoring

Traditional Corn . . . Now Commercialised

Stampkoring has always been an important food in Southern Africa; the whole wheat kernels have been used for sweet puddings and boiled as an accompaniment to meat dishes, similarly to *putu** for generations. This traditional whole kernel corn has now been commercialised under the name of Weet-Rice – the word 'rice' giving the clue to this wheat product's adaptability to all recipes for rice.

Basic recipe for cooking weet-rice: (1) Cook 1 cup well-washed Weet-Rice in 6 cups water to which 1 tablespoon of salt has been added. Cook for at least 30–35 minutes. Rinse with hot water. Steam for another 10–15 minutes. Serves 8 persons.

Milk Method (2): Simmer 5 tablespoons Weet-Rice in $2^3/_4$ cups milk with a vanilla pod until soft and creamy, approximately $1^1/_2$ hours.

Family Weet-Rice Pudding

Lesley's Bokomo Recipe

$2^3/_4$ cups milk, 1 cup uncooked Weet-Rice, $^1/_2$ teaspoon salt, $^1/_4$ cup cream, $^1/_4$ cup butter or margarine, $^1/_2$ cup orange marmalade, vanilla essence. Serves 10 ($^1/_2$ cup servings).

*For *putu*, see *index*.

Heat milk in a 3½ litre (3-quart) saucepan. When milk reaches boiling point, add Weet-Rice and salt gradually and stir until it comes to a full boil. Cover saucepan with a tight lid and simmer about 1½ hours. Remove Weet-Rice from heat and add cream and butter. Fold in orange marmalade. Pour into serving dishes. Serve warm with marmalade sauce.

For the Marmalade Sauce:

1 cup orange marmalade, ⅓ cup sherry, ½ cup chopped nuts.

Melt marmalade with sherry over low heat. Remove from heat and fold in nuts. Serve warm over Weet-Rice pudding.

✻   ✻   ✻

Testing Oven Heat

The Old Way

The time-honoured way of testing the heat of an oven comes in useful with an old-fashioned stove, even today: Place a piece of white paper in the oven.

A very hot oven will turn the paper golden brown in 1 minute.
A hot oven will turn the paper golden brown in 3 minutes.
A moderate oven will turn the paper golden brown in 5 minutes.
A slow oven will turn the paper golden brown in 7 minutes.

Monkey with Turnspit. Sketched from the original coloured manuscript (Flemish, circ. A.D. 1300) by Brenda Lighton with permission of the Trustees of the British Museum.

In South African records less mention is made of cooking by means of the spit than by means of the anthill ovens. Yet when trekking our pioneers found both easily available. Who knows but a baboon might have been used to turn the spit – we have old farmer's tales telling of baboons as *voorlopers*. Surely a baboon who could lead oxen might be trained to turn the meat in common with those dogs in European countries who spent a few hours daily on a tread-mill churning or turning spits – before their reward of buttermilk or bones?

Vegetables

An entry in Van Riebeeck's Diary for October, 1652 reads: *Farewell dinner to the officers of the yacht Goede Hoop. Everything on the table reared at the Cape – fowls, peas, spinach, chervil, asparagus (a finger's thickness) and cabbage, lettuce as hard as cabbages* . . .

Traditional vegetable recipes nearly always need adapting to today's vitamin knowledge, practically no water being used by us for the cooking of green vegetables and, of course, *never ever* bicarbonate of soda for a tempting green colour. Our foremothers, though, did use their ovens for baking vegetables and when vegetables were boiled in 'too much' water they did at least pour the vegetable liquid into the soup pot.

Root vegetables should be put into cold slightly salty water and brought to the boil until tender. Green vegetables go into boiling slightly salty water to be boiled briefly until just tender – never mushy. The art of timing vegetables is learnt when only moisture remains in the cooking pot – no water.

Present-day frozen vegetables are invaluable when fresh vegetables are scarce. To cook, place entire frozen block of vegetables in one or two tablespoons of boiling water and simmer on *lowest* heat, covered. Peas need no water in the pan – which may be buttered. In a few minutes the vegetables will be tender and ready to serve.

Baked Pumpkin

Boer pumpkin (dry not a watery one), butter, sugar, stick cinnamon.

Peel the pumpkin and cut in 7 cm (3") pieces. Place a layer in a baking dish (not glass). Sprinkle sugar over and pats of butter and a few sticks of cinnamon, and bake in oven. Do not use any water.

Curried Green Beans

A Cape Speciality

500 g (1 lb) fresh green beans, 1–2 onions, 1 cup water, salt and pepper, $^3/_4$ cup vinegar, $^1/_3$ cup sugar, 2 teaspoons Maizena (cornflour), $^1/_2$ tablespoon curry powder, or to taste; 2 tablespoons golden syrup, 2 teaspoons mustard.

Cut up the green beans by slicing the Dutch way or shredding, then chop the onions finely. Sauté the chopped onions until yellow and glossy, add the beans and turn a little, then add the water and seasoning. Cook for about 20 minutes or until almost tender. Drain the water, add $^1/_2$ cup of vinegar and the sugar and syrup and mustard, and cook for another 10 minutes. Mix the Maizena and the curry powder with the remainder of the vinegar and simmer for another 10 minutes. Serve hot or cold, as salad.

Stuffed Vine Leaves
Dolmades

> 1 minced onion, 1 kilo (2 lb) minced meat, veal, lamb or pork, or a mixture of two kinds of meat, 1 tablespoon sunflower oil, chopped parsley and dill, 1 small tomato, 2–3 lemons, 1 coffee cup rice, salt and pepper, 2 cubes chicken or meat stock, 750 g (1^1/$_2$ lb) vine leaves, ^{1}/$_2$ cup butter, 2 tablespoons flour, 2 eggs.

Boil minced onion and drain. Place in a bowl onion, minced meat, oil, chopped parsley, dill, and tomato (without seeds), juice of the lemons and rice previously rinsed in cold water, salt and pepper. Melt stock cubes in two cups of hot water. Add some of it in mixture if too thick. Drop leaves in boiling water and boil for two minutes. Spread them face downwards on table and cut stems. Put in each a teaspoon of filling and tuck in edges. Roll into a neat roll.

Line bottom of a large thick saucepan with vine leaves. Arrange dolmades in two layers thickly packed. Cover layers with vine leaves and with a plate turned upside down. Add butter, stock and water enough to cover dolmades. Simmer for 1–1^1/$_2$ hours. Add water when necessary. When ready pan should remain with two glasses of liquid.

Strain liquid and place dolmades in a serving dish. Cover with foil and keep warm. Add liquid, little by little, to the flour, stirring all the time; then bring carefully to the boil and stir until cooked and thick. Remove from heat and add 1 spoon of the hot sauce to the beaten eggs. Stir well. (Always remember – a little hot to the cold mixture first to avoid curdling). Combine egg with rest of the sauce, and spoon sauce carefully over the dolmades. Heat then serve.

Note: The sauce must not boil again.

Sweet Potatoes
The Best are the Borrie ·

The sweet potato (Afrikaans *patat*) is no relation to the *artappel* or ordinary potato; it is of the convolvulas or morning glory family. And what a glorious chestnutty vegetable it is! Traditionally the yellow (*borrie*) potatoes are favoured as they have more flavour than the white watery type. Other ways of using them will be found under *Puddings* and *Ham*.

Grilled Sweet Potatoes
Good for the Braai

Peel and cut lengthwise in halves. Dip in melted butter, sprinkle with salt and sugar. Place on grill below the heat. Cook 10–15 minutes or until brown and tender throughout. Served with grilled ham, sausage, bacon or chops. The potato may be fried in a pan on top of the stove in a mixture of hot butter and cooking oil, drained and crisped before serving.

Sweet-Potato Porcupines
An Entertaining Accompaniment

Peel and slice 1 kg (2 lb) sweet-potatoes. Steam in orange juice and add grated rind, caramel brown sugar and a little butter. Mash until very smooth, season to taste and pipe with a large rose tube into orange shells. Split almonds and slice. Stick these at intervals into the filling and brown lightly under the grill.

Sweet Potato Snacks

Select *borrie* sweet potatoes. Cook them in boiling water until tender. Peel and cut in pieces 5 cm (2″) long. Around each piece wrap a thin slice of bacon and fasten with a toothpick. Place on a pan in a hot oven until the bacon is crisp. Serve with parsley garnish.

Ouma's Glazed Sweet Potatoes

1 kg (2 lb) sweet potatoes, salted water, dried naartjie peel, 3 tablespoons butter, 1 cinnamon stick, 1 cup brown sugar, salt to taste, $^3/_4$ cup water, or $^1/_2$ cup water, $^1/_4$ cup white wine.

Peel and slice the sweet potatoes. Wash in salted water. Place the sweet potatoes in a heavy-bottomed saucepan together with the naartjie peel, butter, stick of cinnamon, brown sugar, salt and water. Simmer gently and when the potatoes are cooked, and the water has boiled away, increase the heat and fry to a golden brown. Remove the cinnamon stick and naartjie peel before serving. Serves 8.

Note: A heavy-bottomed saucepan should be used, or the sweet potatoes tend to burn instead of brown.

Crispy Sweet Potatoes

Sweet potatoes, $^1/_2$ cup brandy, a little golden brown sugar, grated rind of 1 orange, Post Toasties, honey, butter.

Scrub sweet potatoes, using a small nail brush. Cook in skins in salted water. Remove skins when soft. Cut thick slices using a sharp knife. Butter an oven-proof dish and arrange slices flat, but not overlapping. Pour brandy over and sprinkle a little brown sugar and a little honey over all. Grate the rind of an orange all over and crumble Post Toasties over the sweet potatoes. Dot pieces of butter on top, here and there, and place in an oven at 190° C (375° F) for about 20 minutes. This allows the brandy, sugar and butter to melt, but not caramelise. Serve as a dessert with cream or as an accompaniment to roast chicken, pork or mutton.

Glazed Green Onions

12 large green onions, salt, 2 tablespoons butter or margarine, 2 tablespoons brown sugar.

Clean onions, leaving most of the green top on. Cook in boiling salted water to cover in pan for 8 to 10 minutes, or until tender. Drain off water and add butter and sugar. Cook over low heat 8 minutes or until golden brown. Serves 2–3.

Dried Naartjie Peel

That great Malay favourite – naartjie peel is used for flavouring cakes, puddings, meats and vegetables. Dry the naartjie peel either in the sun or in a warming oven. When it is thoroughly dry and hard, put it into an airtight jar and store it for future use. Before use it must be ground in a pestle and mortar until it is a fine powder. A little sugar may be added to this powder before use.

Dry Beans for a Beano

Because of the importance of dried beans today, budget and protein-wise, we give special space to instructions for cooking them, together with some appetising time-honoured recipes.

To cook dry beans: Place 5 cups of cold water with 2 cups of dry beans, bring to the boil slowly and boil for 2 minutes. Remove from heat and allow to soak overnight. Next day, add 2 tablespoons salt and cook over a slow to medium heat. For Cowpea (known as black eye), 30 minutes. Lima and butter beans, 1 hour. Lentils, 1 to 1½ hours. Kidney, navy beans (known as haricot beans), broad beans and soya beans, 2 hours.

The beans can now be seasoned, mixed with lemon juice or tomatoes, and served as a vegetable. They can also be puréed, used in soups and salads, or in a number of unusual dishes.

Bean Casserole

2 cups cooked beans, 500 g (1 lb) minced meat, 1 cup salad oil, 1 cup tomato sauce, 1 packet onion soup mix, 1 teaspoon cider vinegar, 1 teaspoon prepared mustard, pepper to taste, 1 cup water.

Brown the mince in oil. Stir in beans and remaining ingredients. Pour into a casserole, bake uncovered in hot oven 200° C (400° F) for 30 minutes.

Curried Sugar Beans

Pour your favourite curry (see *Index* for Curries) over 250 g (½ lb) tender cooked sugar beans. Mix well and leave for at least half a day before use.

Bean Croquettes

Cooked dry beans such as navy beans, lentils or kidney beans are mashed or sieved, combined with fried, chopped onions, pepper and salt and sufficient breadcrumbs to make the mixture stiff enough to be moulded into balls or flat cakes. Coat them with egg and breadcrumbs and fry in hot deep oil. The croquettes can be served with sauce or brown gravy and garnished with chopped parsley.

Sousboontjies

As Isabelle says . . .

Soak sugar beans overnight. Cook in fresh water until tender. Rinse under tap in colander. Pour back into saucepan. Make a mixture of water, vinegar, salt and sugar to give a tangy sweet/sour taste, pour over and let it cook up. Thicken with a little maizena dissolved in cold water.

Sousboontjies can be served hot or cold and can be kept in the frig. for a long time. (They are ideal for freezing). Use as an accompaniment for meat or as a vegetable. Also spoon on to toast, top with crisp bacon for a lunch or breakfast. Wonderful for taking to a braai! Sousboontjies are delicious with the Sunday leg of mutton and yellow rice. Actually sousboontjies and yellow rice are a *must* for a typical Afrikaans meal.

Soya Barley Cutlets

Our vegetarian students make them all the time!

1-cup cooked soya beans, 1 cup cooked barley, 1 cup wheatgerm, soya sauce, paprika, Knorr Aromat, salt and pepper, fresh tomato purée, breadcrumbs.

Mix the soya beans and barley and rub through a sieve. Add the wheatgerm and seasoning. Shape the mixture into cutlets, press breadcrumbs all round these and fry until golden brown in hot oil. Use a piece of macaroni for the 'bone' or else one of those frilly toothpicks.

Accompaniments:

Baked brinjals (aubergines) with bits of carrot stuck in for faces. Brown mushroom rice. Apples with inside cut out, and an onion inserted in the hole, then baked with a sauce made of margarine, salt, pepper, Knorr Aromat, chopped parsley and sunflower seeds. Baked potatoes with a stuffing of croûtons fried in a curry or garlic sauce.

Note:

For a full book of vegetable recipes refer to our *ABC for Cooks* – which gives recipes for every vegetable grown in South Africa.

✽   ✽   ✽

Flavoured Vinegars

Make Them At Home

Vinegars were an entertaining subject in the old days, giving added interest to many meats. The excellent cheap wine vinegar we buy can be flavoured to gourmet taste with herbs and spices. Place the bruised herbs – such as celery seeds, chillies, tarragon leaves, shallots, garlic – or so on in bottles with hot wine vinegar. Stopper closely. After a few weeks strain the vinegar off into bottles for use.

✽   ✽   ✽

> *Die vrou is die sout van die aarde,*
> *die suurdeeg, beskou op die keper;*
> *Al hoër steeds rys sy in waarde:*
> *Sy's beide die sout en . . . die peper!*

A free literal translation is:

> *A woman is the salt of the earth,*
> *the yeast if under a scope we set her,*
> *Forever increasing in worth,*
> *She's both the salt and . . . the pepper.*

A. G. Visser

'Ricing' to the Occasion

In an old British Settler's record we came across a grumble about the half cooked rice boiled by the slaves and enjoyed by the Cape people. What a feather in our culinary cap! Our Cape Malay way was later endorsed by the Indians who came to Natal about 1859. (Yes, the year South Africa's first railway was begun.) What was it the British settlers didn't like about our rice? It was served every grain separate and not in a British mush. Today the best British restaurants serve it our way.

Fried Rice with Ham and Beans

Budgetwise you can use mealie rice

4 cups cooked, cold rice, 125 g (4 oz) each of ham (shredded) beans (sliced), 1 small onion (chopped), 3 or 4 spring onions, (chopped), 2 tablespoons oil, 1 tablespoon soy sauce, salt and pepper, 2 eggs (beaten), MSG.

Season eggs with salt and pepper to taste and cook as an ordinary omelette in a lightly greased pan. Remove and keep hot. Quick fry the ham with onions and beans for about 20 seconds, stirring all the time; season with soy sauce and simmer for 3 minutes. Add cooked rice, breaking it down with chopsticks to loosen the grains and to heat it through. Slice the omelette, scatter over the rice, sprinkle with spring onions and serve.

Fried Rice with Chicken

As above, substituting 250 g (8 oz) sliced chicken meat for ham and beans.

Fried Rice with Prawns

As above, substituting sliced, fresh prawns for chicken.

Fried Rice with Lobster or Crab

As above, substituting diced lobster or crab for prawns.

Fried Rice with Shrimps and Ham

As above, substituting fresh shrimps and 60 g (2 oz) ham for crab meat.

Savoury Rices

Every family enjoys its own blend of savoury rice made by folding into the hot rice fried onions, tomatoes (skinned) and/or mushrooms, green peppers, etc. with or without grated cheese added.

For Green Rice: Chop fresh (uncooked) parsley finely and combine with the rice (hot or cold). Do not use too much parsley if a too green effect is not desired. Hot butter or garlic butter may be added to this 'parsley' rice.

Traditional Yellow Rice

1 large cup rice, 125 g (4 oz) sugar, $^1/_2$ teaspoon salt, 60 g (2 oz) seeded raisins, 4 cups water, 1 dessertspoon turmeric, 1 tablespoon butter.

Bring the water to the boil. Add all the ingredients except the raisins. Wash the raisins and soak in cold water. Boil the rice about 15 minutes. Strain the raisins and add to the rice. Mix well with a fork. Simmer until rice is cooked. Strain off excess liquid, leave in colander over boiling water until required.

Nut Rice in Orange Cups

Serve with Roast Duck and Other Things

This is an attractive accompaniment to serve with Roast Duck or game birds. It may also accompany pork or lamb.

2 cups chicken broth (bouillon cube with water, milk or stock), 1 cup uncooked rice, 2 tablespoons butter, $^2/_3$ cup pecan nuts (chopped), 2 tablespoons minced parsley, salt to taste; oranges as required.

Combine in a saucepan the chicken broth and the rice. Bring to the boil and stir. Cover and reduce heat and simmer for 15 minutes. Remove from heat. Stir in the butter, nuts and parsley. Season to taste. Take some orange shells, serrating the edges with a sharp knife, and fill with the mixture.

From High Rustenburg Hydro, Stellenbosch we are indebted for the following two tasty and nutritious recipes:

H.R.H. Rice Salad

3 cups cooked brown rice, 3 cups chopped fresh peaches, 1 cup finely chopped celery, $^1/_2$ cup chopped onion, $^1/_2$ cup sunflower seeds, $^1/_2$ cup chopped raisins, $^3/_4$ cup oil, 2 tablespoons lemon juice, 1 teaspoon curry powder, 1 teaspoon soy sauce, 1 teaspoon honey, 3 tablespoons chopped parsley, herb salt to taste.

Combine all ingredients and mix well.

H.R.H. Muesli

Soak in cold water for 8–12 hours:

2 dessertspoons rolled oats, $1^1/_2$ dessertspoons sunflower seeds, 1 dessert-spoon seedless raisins, 1 teaspoon pine kernels, 1 teaspoon millet seeds, 1 teaspoon sesame seeds, chopped dried fruit if desired.

Just before eating add: 1 finely grated apple (peeled), 1 dessertspoon wheat-germ (kept in fridge for freshness), plus other fresh fruits as desired. The wheat germ may be sprinkled on top of each plateful of muesli and the whole decorated with slices of banana.

This dish must be masticated thoroughly to achieve maximum nourishment from minimum quantity. And please note that the overnight soaking of the main ingredients is essential.

Javanese Rijstafel

Nasi Goreng: to serve 8

This famous Javanese dish of fried rice with meat and fish should never have curry powder or tomato added to be ingredients. Here is the way to make it, complete with its accompaniments and sambals. Beer may be drunk with it. (It is eaten with a spoon.)

4 cups Parboiled rice, 5 pints water, 1 tablespoon salt, 1 tablespoon butter, 500 g (1 lb) cooked meat (ham, salt beef or chicken), 4 large onions, 4 leaks, 4 sticks celery, salt, pepper, pinch of sugar, MSG, 1 teaspoon sambal oelek (obtainable at Indian stores), 2 dessertspoons Maggi seasoning, 4 dessertspoons soy sauce, 6 slices bacon (fried crisply), 4 cut-up rock lobster tails, 2 tins shrimps.

Make the rice according to the directions on the packet and allow to cool. Cut the meat into cubes and brown in the oil. Remove and keep warm in a casserole. Chop onions fine and brown in left-over oil. Chop leeks and celery fine and add to the onions, frying all together. Season with salt, pepper, sugar and MSG. Add the oelek, soy sauce and Maggi seasoning. Chop up the crisply fried bacon, rock lobster tails and shrimps and add to above. Now add the rice and, mixing well, fry all together. Decorate with fried eggs or chopped-up rock lobster and omelette made as follows:

Omelette

2 eggs, a knob of butter ($^1/_2$–1 oz), salt and pepper, 2 tablespoons water.

Beat the eggs in a basin. Add a good pinch of salt and pepper, and for each 2 eggs a tablespoon water. Put a knob of butter into your smallest pan. When hot pour in the eggs. Leave for about a minute over a high heat, when the bottom will have set, then loosen the egg mixture from the side of the pan and cook rapidly, tipping the pan from side to side, so that the liquid egg flows underneath and cooks quickly. When the egg is set as you like it – for taste varies – slip your palette knife under the omelette and fold it away from the handle. Grasp the handle firmly and tip on to a hot plate or dish. Do not cook more than 4 eggs in a 6-inch pan, otherwise cooking will take too long and the omelette become dry.

Side Dishes for Nasi Goreng

Pineapple or quince sambal (recipe follows); kroepoek – dried shrimps (obtainable from speciality stores) fried crisply in oil; cucumber salad; browned coconut and an equal amount of peanut butter fried in oil; mango chutney; gherkins; fried whole bananas (dipped in seasoned flour, egg and breadcrumbs and fried in butter); Sate – similar to sosaties (recipe follows).

Pineapple or Quince Sambal

1 medium onion, 3 dessertspoons oil, 1 teaspoon paprika, 1 bayleaf, 1 stick cinnamon, 1 knifepoint oelek (from an Indian store), 1 lb tin pineapple or a tin of quinces, 4 tablespoons pineapple syrup.

Fry all the ingredients (except the pineapple or quince and syrup) in the oil. Strain pineapple and add to above, and add the four tablespoons of syrup.

Nasturtium Seeds

A Time-honoured Substitute for Capers

Gather the nasturtium seeds while they are still young and green; wash them well in cold water, put a little salt with them, and let them soak until next day. Dry the seeds well with a soft cloth, put them into glass bottles, and cover entirely with cold vinegar; 60 g (2 oz) salt, a dozen peppercorns, a small piece of horse-radish, 4 or 5 leaves of tarragon, and 2 cloves may be put with each 1 .25 litres (quart) of vinegar. Cork the bottles securely, and store them in a cool, dry place. The nasturtium seeds will not be ready for some months.

❉   ❉   ❉

Those Good Old Days

They lived without sugar until the 13th century, without coal until 14th century, without butter on their bread until 15th, without tobacco or potatoes until 16th, without tea, coffee or soap until 18th; without trains, telegrams, gas, matches and chloroform until 19th.

Pine Nuts and Raisins in Vine Leaves

With Rice

Cape Town readers might like to surprise their guests with these Turkish canapés from their own garden. At least some of us have the ingredients ready to hand, so why not add this to our South African repertoire of recipes?

³/₄ cup salad oil, 500 g (1 lb) onions (chopped), 2 cups rice, 125 g (4 oz) raisins, 155 g (5 oz) pine nuts, 3 cups water, 2 sprigs thyme, 2 sprigs mint, 1 teaspoon salt, dash of pepper, 12 grape vine leaves, salted (or use spinach or cabbage leaves).

Salt vine leaves in advance, three days before required. Wash and dry selected *young* leaves, sprinkle salt over them and then place leaves on top of each other in layers; weigh down and allow to stand for three days. (About 2 tablespoons of salt will be required for 60 leaves.) Heat salad oil, sauté onions until slightly brown, add rice and continue cooking until rice becomes light brown, too. Add all other ingredients with the exception of the vine leaves. Bring to boil then simmer and continue cooking until all liquid is absorbed. Now reduce heat to a minimum until the rice starts sticking to the bottom of the pan. Remove from heat and extract thyme and mint. Allow to cool in a bowl. Spread leaves out, bottom side up, and on each place 1 tablespoon of the rice mixture. Fold into squares and pack closely together to hold shape in a large shallow pan; place a cover right on top of the leaves with a weight (not too heavy) to hold the little leaf parcels secure while they simmer. When the bottom layer starts to sizzle, pour in 1 tablespoon hot water and shake the pan slightly, returning the lid and weight. Repeat until cooked. Serve hot.

To Dry Your Own Herbs

Collect herbs at full maturity, just before flowering and preferably after a dry spell, on a dry day. If picked on a damp day they will become mildewed.

To dry most herbs, collect them in bunches, tie loosely and suspend from the roof of a dry shed or room. Alternatively, spread the herbs out on slatted shelves in a warm place and turn them daily. Aim to dry them as quickly as possible. Large-leaved herbs can be stripped from their stalks and placed on muslin on a slatted shelf.

Parsley must be washed, shaken well, then placed in a very hot oven at 240° C (475° F) for one minute; it should then be dried like other herbs. When thoroughly dry, the leaves will crackle when grasped, and they can easily be stripped from the stalks. Place the leaves between sheets of greaseproof paper and crush them with a rolling pin; put into small screw-topped jars and label clearly. Store the jars in a cool, dark cupboard.

Parsley Butter

An Old Gardener's Recipe

Here is a use for parsley that has gone to seed. The result is a thin honey. Pack a non-metal saucepan with wet parsley, well washed. Cover with water and boil for 30 minutes. Strain through muslin. Measure and for every 600 ml (1 pint) juice add 3 cups sugar. Boil very quickly until it begins to thicken, then cover and cool and bottle. A little lemon juice may be added to the sugar.

Our Daily Bread,

and the cakes of yesteryear

The very first oven wasn't an oven at all, it was the ubiquitous iron pot used all over the world from the earliest times for stewing, and with a lid on, for baking anything over an open fire. Even bread was baked in the three-legged (Kaffir) pot – which is still a standby among tribal Africans today.

For travellers by oxwagon there was always an ever-ready supply of good ovens in the shape of old antheaps dotted over the veld. Those with the pioneering spirit may be interested to know just how these antheaps were used.

A small deep hole was made at the summit of the ant hill and a large round hole scooped out of the side. Small twigs and dry grass were pushed into the side cavity and set alight. The iron pot or kettle was placed over the hole on top for making coffee or bredie as required.

When the cooking on top was finished, the top hole was plugged, the ashes raked out of the interior, and the loaf of sour-dough bread put into the cavity. The opening was quickly sealed with clay or wet earth 'not antheap soil which is too soft' as one old-timer warned us. After an hour or so the clay was broken and the baked bread removed.

The antheap oven, however, was for the nomads, those who cooked as they trekked. When a family settled and built a house of any size it aspired to a Dutch oven, either a separate clay structure near the house or outside, built on to the kitchen side of the house with a small oven door opening at the side of the hearth. It had no chimney. Even when metal stoves with fires beneath were introduced, the supplementary Dutch oven had its own special uses when quantities of bread were required, such as that at Genadendal, where we were told not so long ago that the Moravian Church still made batches of Communion Bread – in their case, a form of unleavened bun.

To heat the Dutch oven ready for its batch of bread, the fire of charcoal or wood was lit, and the fire stoked for an hour or so. The ashes were then quickly raked out and the already risen loaves (in tins or without) deftly placed in position in the oven by means of the *broodskop,* a broad blade with handle. The oven door was shut and usually sealed with clay to exclude air vents. When the bread was baked the loaves were retrieved from the ashes and anything that required a mild heat placed inside; for example, at the Drostdy at Swellendam Dr Cook told us that bush tea was dried out in the huge oven there for the use of the entire household. In the Koopmans de Wet Museum (Strand Street, Cape Town), is a beautiful example of a Dutch oven, with a 'smoking loft' above.

Suurdeeg – Sourdough
Hilda Gerber's

This is the yeast that gave rise to *suurdeeg* bread – so often mentioned in old cookery books:

Take 1¹/₂ large breakfast cups of boiling water and a breakfast cup of cold water, a little salt and enough flour to make a thick paste. First stir the flour with the cold water and then add the boiling water to it. Cover the dish with a warm cloth and place it in a 'cool' oven or by the side of the fire until it sours. Generally speaking 300 ml (¹/₂ pint) liquid yeast is equal to one cube of fresh yeast, or one sachet – one heaped teaspoon – of dried yeast.

Mealiemeal Yeast
An Old Farm Recipe for Bread

Take 3 cups of boiling milk, potato or rice water or plain boiling water, and pour over 1¹/₂ cups of dry mealiemeal; stir well to mix, cover and leave in a warm place overnight. Mix well with 1¹/₂ cups of very hot water, one tablespoon of sugar, and as much salt as you require for your bread. Stir in enough flour to make a fairly stiff sponge, beat it very thoroughly, cover and stand in a warm place until it becomes very bubbly. It usually takes about 1¹/₂ hours in warm weather.

Now knead in as much flour as you require to make your dough, and when thoroughly kneaded leave to prove. Knead well, make into loaves and when risen to twice their size they must be baked at once in a hot oven. This method is very easy and reliable, and the bread is always sweet and nice, though in the winter it is a bit slow as a rule.

Bread

Thanks to our Government subsidy, baker's bread, especially the brown loaf, is wholesome 'budget' food value. Confectioner's bread, made by hand in a variety of flavours and shapes costs two to three times as much so actually in our opinion should be classified as 'cake'. It is said that when Marie Antoinette suggested that the peasants eat cake if they had no bread, she referred to unleavened bread – without yeast – of her native Austria, popularly called cake. She was blamed for so much why attribute so nonsensical a remark to an educated – if pampered and misguided – woman?

Wholewheat Bread
Silwood Kitchen's Detailed Instructions

Home-made wholewheat bread is most delicious when freshly baked and spread with butter, honey or cheese. Stored correctly it keeps extremely well and can be served up to a week after baking. For variation the loaves may be baked in well-greased flower pots, or shaped into cottage loaves on a baking sheet.

To make cheese bread, add 340 g (12 oz) of finely grated Cheddar or any hard cheese to the flour with the yeast mixture.

1¹/₂ teaspoons butter, 30 g (1 oz) yeast, 1 teaspoon brown sugar, 3³/₄ cups plus 4 teaspoons lukewarm water, 12 cups stone-ground wholewheat flour, 1 tablespoon salt, 2 tablespoons honey or golden syrup, 1 tablespoon Sunflower oil, 4 tablespoons chopped nuts if required.

Grease four 500 g (1 lb) loaf tins with the butter. Crumble the yeast into a small bowl and mash in the brown sugar with a kitchen fork. Add 4 teaspoons of water and cream the water, sugar and yeast together to form a smooth paste. Set the bowl aside in a warm, draught-free place for 15–20 minutes, or until the yeast has risen and is puffed up and frothy.

Put the flour and salt into a warmed, large mixing bowl. Make a well in the centre of the flour mixture and pour in the yeast, the honey, the remaining lukewarm water and the oil. Using your fingers, or a spatula, gradually draw the flour into the liquid. Continue mixing until all the flour is incorporated and the dough comes away from the sides of the bowl. Turn the dough out on to a floured board or marble slab and knead for about 10 minutes, reflouring the surface if the dough becomes sticky. The dough should then be elastic and smooth. Rinse, thoroughly dry and lightly grease the large mixing bowl. Shape the dough into a ball and return it to the bowl. Dust the top of the dough with a little flour and cover the bowl with a clean, damp cloth. Set the bowl in a warm, draught-free place and leave it for one to one and a half hours, or until the dough has risen and almost doubled in bulk.

Turn the risen dough out of the bowl on to a floured surface and knead vigorously for about 10 minutes. Using a sharp knife, cut the dough into four pieces. Roll and shape each piece into a loaf. Place the loaves in the tins. If you prefer a country-style loaf, use a heated, sharp knife or kitchen scissors to make a deep gash on the top of each loaf and then dust them with a little wholewheat flour. Cover the tins with a damp cloth and return to a warm place for 30 to 45 minutes, or until the dough has risen to the top of the tins.

Preheat oven to very hot 240° C (475° F). Place the tins in the centre of the oven and bake for 15 minutes. Then lower the oven temperature to hot 225° C (430° F), put the bread on a lower shelf in the oven and bake for another 25 to 30 minutes. After removing the bread from the oven, tip the loaves out of the tins and rap the underside with your knuckles. If the bread sounds hollow like a drum, it is cooked. If the bread does not sound hollow, lower the oven temperature to 190° C (375° F), return the loaves, upside down to the oven and bake for a further 10 minutes. Cool the loaves on a wire rack.

Variation: For nut loaves add 4 tablespoons chopped nuts (even peanuts).

Today's Health Bread

800 g (1 lb 12 oz) nutty wheat flour, or stone-ground whole wheat, 140 g (4^1/$_2$ oz) rolled oats, 140 g (4^1/$_2$ oz) wheat germ, 90 g (3 oz) each soya flour and bran, 50 ml (2 fluid oz) honey, 50 ml (2 fluid oz) oil, 1 tablespoon salt, 2 cakes of yeast, about 1 litre (4 cups) warm water.

Place all dry ingredients in a large bowl, add the honey and oil, dissolve the yeast in 1 cup of the water and add to the dry ingredients with enough of the warm water to give the dough a dropping consistency. Lightly oil three 1 kg (2 lb) loaf tins and divide the mixture into three. Cover and leave to rise for an hour. This should bring the dough to the top of the tin, when it is ready for baking. Bake the bread in a pre-set oven for about an hour. Molasses may be added instead of honey.

❋   ❋   ❋

Not only our Voortrekkers set bread to rise under their beds. Most pioneers did the same. *Surleas* bread derived from old French 'sur lit'.

Fresh Mealie Bread

2 cups minced mealies (from the cob), 2 large tablespoons butter, $^1/_4$–$^1/_2$ cup sugar, 2 eggs, salt to taste, sufficient milk to bring the mixture to the consistency of a thin batter, 1 teaspoon baking powder. (2 tablespoons cooking oil may be used instead of the butter.)

Mix the mealies and butter together. Add the sugar, well-beaten eggs, salt and milk. Lastly add the baking powder. Stir well. Pour the mixture into a greased pudding bowl and steam as you would a pudding, for $1^1/_2$ hours. This mixture should have the appearance of a soft batter. Serve with lavish helpings of butter with roasts, stews, braaivleis – in fact, any meat course, or serve slices, warm or cold, with butter, syrup or honey.

Banana Bread

$1^1/_4$ cups cake flour, $^1/_2$ cup sugar, $^1/_2$ teaspoon salt, 1 teaspoon baking soda, $^1/_2$ cup solid vegetable shortening, 2 fully ripe medium bananas, 2 eggs.

Sift dry ingredients into bowl. Whirl remaining ingredients in blender to form an emulsion. Add to dry ingredients and mix just until dry ingredients are moistened. Spoon into lightly buttered and floured square pan and bake in moderate oven 180° C (350° F) 35 to 40 minutes. Remove from oven and let stand in pan 5 minutes. Loosen edges with spatula and turn out onto cake rack covered with waxed paper. Cool to room temperature before cutting in squares.

To Make without Blender: Add shortening to sifted dry ingredients and cut in as for piecrust. Purée bananas and add with well-beaten eggs. Proceed as directed.

This is a very moist, spongy bread that stays fresh several days if stored airtight.

The Mosbolletjie

Introduced by the French refugees who came to settle in the Franschhoek district of the Cape in 1688, mosbolletjies have been eaten with delight and nostalgia ever since. Country and town bakers still make them and many housewives, true to family tradition, are proud of their own baking. The word *mosbolletjie* comes from *mos,* the juice of the grape in its first stages of fermentation and *bolletjie* a bun.

During the wine-making season the freshly fermented grape juice is commonly used instead of yeast. But any yeast can be made for use in mosbolletjies, although they are only entitled to their name if the correct rising-*mos* is used. An old-timer who made her own *mos* describes her method:

Mos may be made with fresh grapes or raisins, whichever is most convenient. To make it with fresh grapes, take a clean preserve jar and fill it with as many crushed grapes as it will hold. White grapes will make whiter bread and buns. Cover the jar and stand in a warm place for a few days until it begins to bubble. Let it ferment well but before it begins to turn sour, strain off the liquid and use as required.

When using raisins, mince 30 g (1 oz) of raisins finely and put them in a preserve jar with a pint of warm water. Stand in a warm place until it ferments

– that is, when the raisins rise to the top. It usually takes 3–4 days, as the dried grapes do not ferment as readily as the fresh ones. Strain.

If intending to use *mos* yeast regularly for your bread, do not wash out the jar after removing the liquid – the slight amount left on the sides will cause the second lot to ferment in a far shorter time. But, of course, if the jar should be sour it must be washed before use. Although *mos* is a reliable yeast, at the same time it is the easiest to spoil, because if not used at the right moment the juice turns to vinegar.

Rusks of Mosbolletjies

When mosbolletjies are cold, either break them in halves lengthwise or across and dry them in a warm oven, turning frequently. The rusks should be thoroughly dried out to the centre and have an even golden colour. They should be broken, not cut, to give them the traditional feathery appearance.

The Recipe for Mosbolletjies

2 kg (4 lb) flour, 250 g ($^1/_2$ lb) butter, 500 g (1 lb) sugar, 7 g ($^1/_4$ oz) aniseed, 600 ml (1 pint) mos, 600 ml (1 pint) warm milk.

Take $^1/_3$ of the flour, place in your mixing bowl and make a well in the centre, pour in the mos and mix to a soft sponge. Cover closely and leave in a warm place to rise for about 8 hours. Melt the butter in the warm milk and leave until lukewarm, add the liquid and the rest of the flour to the sponge and knead it well – salt may be added if liked. The dough must be firm. Allow to rise overnight after covering it very warmly – a chill is fatal – add the sugar and spice and knead again very thoroughly; the more you knead the lighter your buns will be. Make into buns of a uniform size and of a long roll shape. Stand them on end and pack very closely together in the baking tin so that they will rise high and not wide. Leave to rise to double their size, brush the tops with beaten egg and milk and sprinkle with sugar. Bake in a very hot oven.

Boerebeskuit

Rusks with Yeast

1 kg (2 lb) butter, 3 cups warm milk, 1$^1/_2$ tablespoons salt, 2 cakes of yeast, 1 tablespoon sugar, 5 kg (10 lb) flour or fine grade wholemeal, 3–4 egg yolks, $^1/_2$ cup milk, 1 cup sugar.

Optional Flavouring: 1 teaspoon ground cinnamon, 1 grated nutmeg.

Melt butter and add milk which has been warmed. Add sugar, salt and yeast, and, if you wish, any of the flavouring suggested above. Make into a stiff dough with the flour or meal and add more flour if necessary. Knead well. Form into buns and put into greased pans. Cover and let rise in a warm place until double in bulk. Beat egg yolks and mix with $^1/_2$ cup milk. Brush over top of buns. Bake in centre of oven at 200° C (400° F) for 15–20 minutes. When cold, break in pieces and dry out in a cool oven. The finished product should be uniform and a light creamy colour.

Baking Powder Tip. For best results buy small tins of baking powder, keep lid tightly closed and replenish often.

Buttermilk Rusks

10 cups sifted flour, 500 g (1 lb) butter (or half butter and half margarine), 3 eggs, 1 carton buttermilk (2 cups), 1 tablespoon bicarbonate of soda, 1 tablespoon baking powder, 1 tablespoon cream of tartar, 2–2¹/₂ cups sugar, 1 teaspoon salt.

Rub the shortening into the well-sifted dry ingredients, and add the sugar. Beat the eggs and buttermilk together, and add to the dry ingredients. With a tablespoon, make heaps to resemble scones and bake in a hot oven at 200° C (400° F), as you would scones, for about 20 minutes, or until cooked. Remove and cool a little. Divide the scones into two, using two forks. Place on pans in the oven 130° C (250° F) to dry out slowly. Yield: a big family batch to store for the weeks to come.

Silwood's Scones

The Basic Recipe

2 cups self-raising flour, 1 tablespoon sugar, 1 egg, 1 small teaspoon salt, a little milk, 1 tablespoon butter.

Sieve the flour and salt together, add the sugar. Rub in the butter and mix to a light dough with a well-beaten egg and a little milk. Roll out 12 mm (¹/₂″) thick and bake in a very quick oven for about 10 minutes. Sour cream used in place of the shortening, improves the scones.

Water or water and milk may be used instead of whole milk. Ice-cold water results in a very light 'dry' scone that keeps well and is particularly effective when cheese is used for savoury scones.

Cheese Scones: Use standard recipe as above plus ¹/₂ cup or more grated mature (strong) Cheddar cheese and a pinch of mustard powder and one beaten egg.

Tea Scones: Add 1–2 tablespoons sugar and 1 beaten egg.

Fruit Scones: Add to tea scone recipe ¹/₂ cup mixed fruit or 1 cup sultanas or raisins.

Date Scones: Add to tea scone recipe ¹/₂ cup cut-up dates.

Pumpkin Scones

Mrs Hutchon's

Take 2 cups flour, 1 cup mashed pumpkin, 1 tablespoon butter, 2 tablespoons sugar, 1 egg, 2 teaspoons baking powder, enough milk to make a soft dough.

Beat butter and sugar till creamy, add egg, and beat well, then beat in mashed pumpkin, then flour, and enough milk to make a soft dough. Roll out, cut, and bake in hot oven.

Lesley advises: Scones are nicest freshly made, but if you do have some left over you can freshen them up by wrapping them securely in aluminium foil and popping them in a very hot oven 230° C (450° F) for about 10 minutes.

Buttermilk Date Scones

2 cups bread flour (or ¹/₂ nutty snowflake and ¹/₂ white flour), 2 tablespoons butter, 1 egg, 2 teaspoons cream of tartar, 1 teaspoon bicarbonate of soda, a pinch of salt, ³/₄ cup chopped dates*, buttermilk.

Sift all the dry ingredients together. Rub in the butter, beat the egg and add to the buttermilk. Mix lightly. Roll out and cut into desired shapes. Bake at 200° C (400° F) for 10 minutes.

*Cut dates with scissors dipped in hot water instead of using a knife.

Note: When using buttermilk always reduce the cream of tartar by half. Instead of the usual proportion (2 parts cream of tartar to 1 part bicarbonate of soda), when buttermilk is used, take 1 part bicarbonate of soda to 1 part cream of tartar. The same principle applies when using sour cream.

Oblietjies ... Wafers

Among the culinary utensils of museum kitchens of the Cape (Groot Constantia, Tulbagh and the Drostdy, Swellendam) you'll see many *oblietjieysters* – lidded, iron pans with long handles. Dr Mary Cook, the curator of the Drostdy Museum at Swellendam, told us that Mrs Hannah Rothman, after research, had concluded that *oblietjie* was derived from the Latin *oblatus* and the French *oblation* (offering to God). Apparently the Huguenot wafers were similar to those taken at communion. We had often wondered why so much wine was used in the old recipes!

These *oblietjie* irons brought with them by the Huguenots in 1688 were specifically used for *oblietjies,* waferlike pancakes, rolled with open ends, roly-poly style or trumpet shaped, immediately on removal from the pan. If you wish to try out this Huguenot tea-time treat today, cook the batter as a pancake or crumpet on a griddle or a greased hot plate of the stove.

Oblietjies – or Oubliés

Hildagonda Duckitt's Recipe

1 kg (2 lb) fine flour, 500 g (1 lb) castor sugar, 375 g ($^3/_4$ lb) butter, 4 eggs, 2 dessertspoons fine sifted cinnamon, 1 cup wine.

Beat butter to a cream, mix with the sugar; add eggs, whisked separately, the wine, and lastly the flour, in which the cinnamon has been mixed. If the batter is not quite thin enough to spread, add a little more wine. Bake in a heated *oublié*-pan: put about a dessertspoonful on pan, shut tight and hold over the fire to brown on both sides; it will take two minutes. Open the pan, roll the *oublié* as you would a pancake, while hot. The *oubliés* ought to be very crisp and light, and as thin as a wafer.

Pancakes

Pancakes, traditionally speaking, were served in England on Shrove Tuesday (the Tuesday immediately preceding Ash Wednesday) 'pancake day'. The Cape Malays celebrate the cutting of a baby's first tooth with a pancake party. The tossing of pancakes is fun for all – except she who has to clear up afterwards.

3 eggs, $1^1/_2$ cups flour, pinch of salt, 3 tablespoons melted butter, 3 tablespoons brandy or rum, 2 cups milk (water or soda water).

Break the eggs into a wide jug. Beat well with the brandy. Sift in the dry ingredients. Mix in the milk and lastly the melted butter. Pour on to hot oil and butter mixture in a frying pan. When bubbles appear toss to the other side.

Sheeptail Fat and 'Tall Tales'

One of the chief cooking joys of our great-grandmothers and their grand-mothers before them, was sheeptail fat. Not only was it used to spread on bread but it was used for all cooking where fat was needed. This was the fat that worked miracles for cakes, cookies, pastries and deep-fried foods and was cherished right down to its remnant *kaaings* –which old-timers tell us they chewed 'like toffee' on their way to school.

The fat-tailed sheep of the Cape appear to have been one of the minor wonders of the world in the old days before the merinos took over. These hardy creatures, with more hair than wool to their coats, survived where other sheep hadn't a hope. The mutton was superb and as for those fat tails – there is many an old story. One old farmer told us that he had heard of tails so large that they had to be specially supported with a wooden crutch. Like the bushwomen's protruding posteriors, the tails were Nature's way of providing a built-in food bank for times of drought.

Kaiingkoekies

4 cups flour, 2 cups kaaiings (rendered mutton tail fat, little pieces left over), 2 cups sugar, 1 cup butter, 1 teaspoon bicarbonate of soda, 2 tea-spoons cream of tartar, 2 teaspoons ground cinnamon, a little dried naartjie peel (ground), 1 egg.

Mix to right consistency to roll out and cut 3 mm ($^1/_8''$) thick. Cook like biscuits.

Sweet Potato Waffles

To every 2 rounded tablespoons of mashed potatoes, add 1 level tablespoon of butter, 1 of sugar, 250 ml (1 cup) of milk and 4 level tablespoons of flour. Beat all well together and add an egg, well beaten. Bake in waffle iron and serve with butter.

South African Crumpets

Similar to English Pancakes

Beat 1 egg with 1 tablespoon sugar or honey until light and fluffy, then add 5 tablespoons sifted cake flour and 1 tablespoon of melted butter. Mix together, then gradually add enough buttermilk to make a dropping con-sistency (about 2 tablespoons). Set this mixture aside for 1 hour, then stir in 2 teaspoons of baking powder. Mix well and drop spoonfuls of mixture on to hot greased girdle. When bubbles appear, turn crumpet and cook on other side. Serve with a dollop of whipped cream, topped with your favourite jam or preserve. Or serve hot from girdle spread with butter, topped with honey.

Soetkoekies

In the old days at Christmas time, red stripes were put into these soet-koekies by adding the red bolus last, and stirring or mixing it into the kneaded dough so that the bolus was visible in streaks – that is, not mixed so well that the bolus disappears. The effect is similar to that of a 'marbled' cocoa or chocolate cake.

2 kg (4 lb) flour, 1.4 kg (3 lb) caramel brown sugar, *or* 1.2 kg (2¹/₂ lb) sugar and 4 full tablespoons golden syrup, 1 tablespoon bicarbonate of soda, 500 g (1 lb) butter, 1 teaspoon red bolus (obtainable from chemists), 250 g (¹/₂ lb) lard or tail fat, 1 tablespoon cloves, 4 eggs, well beaten, 1 cup sherry, 1 tablespoon ginger, 2 teaspoons salt, 2 tablespoons cinnamon.

Mix the butter and lard with the flour. Add all the remaining ingredients, including the eggs and sherry (but not the red bolus). Make a stiff dough and knead well. Mix in the red bolus, as described above. Leave overnight. Next day, roll out thinly, cut into rounds and bake in a moderate oven.

Vetkoek

Truly Traditional

'Vetkoek' remains a favourite with South Africans today, especially at braaivleis functions. It is generally eaten instead of bread and is served with jam or syrup. In the old days the fat was usually sheeptail fat. Today we use cooking fat or oil.

1.2 kg (2¹/₂ lb) cake flour, 1 sachet active dried yeast, 1 teaspoon salt, 1 teaspoon sugar.

Dissolve sugar in half a cup of luke-warm water. Sprinkle active dried yeast on surface. Let stand for 5–10 minutes. Mix salt with flour, make a well in the centre of flour in the mixing bowl, now pour in the sugar and yeast liquid. Scoop flour around and mix lightly, then add more hand-warm water till a dough of scone consistency is formed. Knead. Pat down gently and smooth over the top with a tablespoon of very soft butter or margarine. Let rise till doubled in size. Knead and 'knock' down gently and let rise again. Roll pieces the size of a plum between the palms of the hands and drop into hot cooking oil. (The oil is hot enough when a small piece of dough dropped into it comes to the surface immediately.

Three Delicious Ways to Serve 'Vetkoek'

Pre-cooked minced meat can be mixed in the dough before frying the vetkoek. Or cut open the vetkoek while still warm, butter and use a filling of pilchards and tomato.

This is delicious with a layer of grated cheese, or cheese and vienna sausages – or syrup or honey after vetkoek has been buttered.

Try it with a sugar and cinnamon mixture.

Sheeptail fat came in abundance from fat-tailed sheep. Some tails weighed from 10–15 kg (20–30 lb) each.

Koeksisters . . . Koesisters

Who said that the word *koeksister* or *koesister* had anything to do with a sister? It is, of course, an onomatopoetic Afrikaans word describing the *siss* or sizzle of the hot dough in the cold syrup. Originally from Batavia, this traditional old Dutch sweetmeat is still popular today, especially with those who have a sweet tooth. Koeksister is the approved Afrikaans spelling. When Malays speak of koeksisters they mean bollas. These are made like koeksisters but are round and rolled in sugar and green and red coconut. The Malays call our koeksisters 'twisties'.

Our Koeksisters

With Yeast

1 teaspoon dry yeast, $^1/_2$ cup luke-warm water, 1 tablespoon sugar, $^1/_4$ teaspoon salt, $2^1/_2$ cups flour, 1 egg, 2 tablespoons butter *or* margarine, $^1/_4$ cup sugar.

Dissolve 1 tablespoon sugar in $^1/_2$ cup luke-warm water and allow to stand for 15 minutes. Melt the butter. Beat the egg and the $^1/_4$ cup sugar, then add to the melted butter. Beat very well. Add the yeast mixture to the egg mixture, and then add the flour and salt. Add sufficient luke-warm water to make a fairly stiff dough. Knead very well, cover with a warm, damp cloth to avoid drying out of dough, and allow to rise for approximately 1 hour. Roll out the dough to 6 mm ($^1/_4''$) thickness and cut into strips, then plait. Fry in deep, hot oil, in an enamel pot, then plunge into *ice-cold* syrup.

For the Syrup:

8 cups sugar, 6 cups water, 4 cinnamon sticks, 3 pieces naartjie peel, 6 cloves.

Boil all the ingredients together, and allow to cool to ice cold.

In order to keep a supply of chilled syrup, use half the syrup at a time, keeping the second half in a refrigerator, then halfway through change over. In this way, the syrup can be used over and over again.

Never store koeksisters in a closed container as this makes them soggy. The oil should be strained and stored away for future use in sweet dishes.

Koeksisters

With Baking Powder

4 cups flour, 3 teaspoons baking powder, 1 teaspoon salt, 2 tablespoons butter or margarine, 1 tablespoon sugar, 2 eggs, about 1 cup water.

Sift the flour, baking powder and salt into a large bowl. Rub in the butter or margarine, add the sugar, and moisten with the beaten eggs and water to make a soft dough. Knead very well and leave to rest – overnight if possible – covered with a damp cloth. Next day, roll out very thinly. Cut into strips 2.5 cm (1'') wide and 3.5 cm ($1^1/_2''$) long and cut these in three up to near the end, and plait together loosely; then drop into deep hot oil (about 3 bottles). The temperature is correct when a small piece of dough dropped into the centre of pan rises immediately to the top again. (The oil must not be too hot). Drop koeksisters in and keep turning. When light brown, drop immediately into ice-cold syrup. Drain on a rack over a tray to catch droplets.

Note: Use two spoons – both with holes in them – one for removing from the oil and the other from the sugar syrup to avoid making the syrup oily.

The Syrup

6 cups sugar, 3 cups water, $^1/_2$ teaspoon cream of tartar mixed with a little water, 3 or 4 pieces of stick cinnamon or a few pieces of ginger, or lemon juice and grated rind to taste.

Dissolve the sugar slowly in the water then allow to boil. Add the cream of tartar, mixed with as little water as possible, some stick cinnamon, ginger, or lemon juice and grated rind (to taste). Boil rapidly for 10 minutes, cool and chill in the refrigerator.

The Secret of Success: The syrup must be kept chilled throughout dipping period. Divide syrup in half, keep one half in refrigerator while other is in use and keep exchanging as the syrup warms.

Beestings Cake
Made with Yeast

The day a cow calved many a farmer's wife used to seize the opportunity to make a beestings cake; the beestings (or more correctly 'beest') usually being the third milking from a mammal, in this case the cow, and it was used for the custard filling of this yeast cake. If you don't live where cows calve you can substitute ordinary milk in the custard. The following is made with dried yeast.

500 g (1 lb) flour. Sift $^1/_2$ cup of the flour into a slightly warmed basin. Sprinkle 2 teaspoons (one sachet) dry yeast over it. Make a well in the flour and pour into it $^1/_2$ cup mixed lukewarm water and milk. Add $1^1/_2$ teaspoons sugar and stir until blended. Cover and leave to rise in a warm place for 20 minutes. Cream $^1/_2$ cup butter and $^1/_2$ cup sugar, and add $^1/_2$ teaspoon salt, 1 teaspoon grated lemon rind, $1^1/_2$ tablespoons lemon juice, 2 beaten eggs, 1 teaspoon vanilla essence and $^1/_2$ cup water and milk mixed. Mix well.

Stir part of the flour into the butter mixture and knead in the rest. Then add the yeast mixture and knead dough well. Cover and allow to rise in a warm place until it has doubled in bulk. Then shape the dough as desired and put into a round cake tin. Leave for about 20 minutes to rise.

Topping: Meanwhile combine $^1/_2$ cup of sugar, $^1/_4$ cup butter, $^1/_4$ cup milk, $^1/_4$ cup honey and $^1/_2$ cup chopped, blanched almonds. Stir over a slow heat until the mixture reaches boiling point. Allow to cool slightly. Pour this over the prepared dough and bake in a moderate oven for about 20 minutes. Remove from the pan and allow to cool. Cut in half and sandwich together with Beestings Custard.

Beestings Custard

600 ml (1 pint) beestings (third milking after a calf is born) or just use ordinary milk and 3 eggs, 2 tablespoons sugar, 3 eggs, 1 tablespoon corn-flour (moistened with a little milk), vanilla, salt to taste.

Pour the milk into the top section of a double boiler, add the salt, sugar, eggs, cornflour (moistened with a little milk) and vanilla essence, and cook until thick, stirring with a metal spoon. Allow the mixture to cool, then use as a filling for the beestings cake.

Beesting Cake

With Baking Powder

Here is a recipe for beesting cake using ordinary milk, instead of real beestings and baking powder instead of yeast. Cream 90 g (3 oz) butter with 60 g (2 oz) sugar. Beat in 1 egg till smooth. Sift together 2 cups flour, 2 teaspoons baking powder and $^1/_2$ teaspoon salt. Add alternately to the batter, with 2 tablespoons milk. Turn the batter into a greased and floured 20 cm springform pan.

Spread the following topping over the cake.

Melt 90 g (3 oz) butter and add 125 g (4 oz) sugar. Add 1 cup chopped ground almonds, 2 tablespoons milk and 1 teaspoon vanilla. Bring the ingredients to the boil and cool. Bake the cake in a moderately hot oven, about 220° C (425° F) for about 25 minutes.

Cool the cake and cut through the middle, then fill the centre with beestings custard. This is made in the top of a double boiler, follow recipe as above.

Easy Sandwich Cake

2 eggs, 2 teaspoons baking powder, $^1/_4$ teaspoon vanilla, 1 cup sugar, $^1/_2$ cup milk, 1 cup flour, $^1/_4$ teaspoon salt, butter size of an egg.

Beat sugar and eggs together. Add flour sifted with baking powder and salt. Add vanilla. Put milk with butter on stove and heat until they foam together and let come to the boil. Add to mixture while hot. Pour into two sandwich tins and bake 12 to 15 minutes in moderately hot oven. Sandwich with jam.

Ye Old Sweet Potato Cake

2 cups mashed sweet potatoes, $^1/_2$ cup butter, 2 eggs, $^3/_4$ cup sugar, juice of $^1/_2$ lemon, 1 teaspoon nutmeg or cinnamon, $1^1/_2$ cups flour, 2 teaspoons baking powder, $^1/_2$ cup milk, 1 teaspoon salt.

Add the butter and beaten eggs to the potato while still hot; add the sugar, salt and nutmeg or cinnamon. Sift together the flour and baking powder and add to the potato alternately with the wilk. Add the lemon juice, pour into a greased pan. Bake in a moderate oven.

Silwood's Papaw Cake

$1^1/_2$ cups flour, 1 cup mashed papaw, $^1/_2$ cup sugar, 1 egg, 1 teaspoon vanilla essence, 2 level teaspoons baking powder, 125 g (4 oz) butter, pinch of salt, $^1/_2$ cup milk.

Cream butter, egg yolk and sugar well together; add the papaw. Sift together all dry ingredients and add alternately with the milk to the butter mixture. Lastly add well-beaten egg white. Fill into a 20 cm (8'') sandwich tin and bake in a moderate oven for approximately $^3/_4$ hour at 180° C (350° F). Cool, split and fill with mashed papaw and a little whipped cream. Sprinkle with icing sugar and serve immediately.

Moist, Sticky Gingerbread

Old Fashioned as Made at Silwood Kitchen

1 egg, ¹/₂ cup brown sugar, ¹/₂ cup sour milk (or ¹/₂ cup buttermilk), ¹/₂ cup syrup, 1 teaspoon bicarbonate of soda, 2 teaspoons ground ginger, 1 teaspoon mixed spice, 2 tablespoons butter, 1¹/₂ cups flour, 2 tablespoons mixed fruit (optional), 2 tablespoons chopped walnuts and a little chopped preserved ginger (optional), a pinch salt.

Sift dry ingredients together. Beat egg and sugar together until light. Melt slowly together in a pot the syrup and butter, add milk and pour into mixture. Add fruit and nuts. Pour into a greased and paper-lined loaf pan 20 cm x 10 cm (8″ x 4″). Bake in an oven heated to 180° C (350° F) for 45 minutes.

Lesley's Seed Cake

This was a great favourite when our Irish granny was young. It was offered to the women visitors with a glass of port if they called in the afternoon. To drink wine on its own would not have been considered respectable.

1 cup butter or half butter and half margarine, 1 cup castor sugar, 4 eggs, 3 cups flour, 1 teaspoon baking powder, a pinch of salt, 1 dessertspoon caraway seeds (or to taste), 1 tablespoon Irish whiskey *or* 1 teaspoon vanilla essence, extra caraway seeds to dust the top.

Cream the butter and sugar together until white and fluffy. Add the eggs, one at a time, with a teaspoon of flour. Sift the remaining flour with the salt and baking powder, and fold gently into the egg mixture with the caraway seeds. Add the whisky or vanilla essence, and pour the mixture into a 20 cm (8″) greaseproof paper-lined tin. Scatter some caraway seeds on top, and bake at 190° C (375° F) for one hour. Reduce the heat towards the end of the baking time.

Variation: If you don't like caraway seeds, you can add 1¹/₂ cups of sultanas instead.

Settlers' Madeira Cake

Madeira Cake, we are assured, didn't originate on the island – it got its name from being served with the wine of that name.

1 cup butter, grated rind of ¹/₂ lemon, pinch ground cinnamon, 1¹/₄ cups castor sugar, 5 eggs, 3¹/₄ cups flour, a pinch of salt, 1 teaspoon baking powder, ¹/₂ cup milk, slice of citron peel.

Prepare a 20 cm (8″) cake tin. Grease the tin and line the bottom with greaseproof paper and then grease again. Cream the butter with the lemon rind and cinnamon, add sugar and beat until the mixture is light and soft. Beat the eggs one at a time with a small spoonful of the flour, then sift the remaining flour with the baking powder and salt and fold into the mixture with the milk. Turn into the prepared tin and bake in a moderate oven at 180° C (350° F) for about 1¹/₂ hours. After the first ¹/₂ hour place a slice of citron peel on the top of the cake and after 1 hour reduce the heat to 170° C (325° F).

Silwood Fruit Cake

500 g (1 lb) butter, 10 eggs, 500 g (1 lb) castor sugar, $^1/_2$ teaspoon salt, 250 g (8 oz) lemon peel, 750 g (1$^1/_2$ lb) flour, 1 teaspoon mixed spice, 1 kg (2 lb) sultanas, 125 g ($^1/_4$ lb) cherries, 1 kg (2 lb) raisins, 1 teaspoon nutmeg, 1 kg (2 lb) currants, 8 oz (500 g) almonds, 300 ml ($^1/_2$ pint) brandy.

Cream the butter, sugar and salt, then add the eggs singly, beating for 5 minutes after each. (Add a little flour if it curdles.) Mix the fruit, chopped peel and cherries together, floured a little. Add spices to the flour; add all to the beaten eggs, butter and sugar. Add brandy. Mix well. Put in a 30 cm (12") tin lined with paper. Bake at 150° C (300° F) for 3–4 hours.

Dundee Cake

250 g ($^1/_2$ lb) butter or margarine, 1 cup castor sugar, 5–6 eggs, 2 cups flour, pinch of salt, 125 g (4 oz) currants, 125 g (4 oz) raisins, 125 g (4 oz) sultanas, 60 g (2 oz) chopped candied peel, 90 g (3 oz) ground almonds, the zest of one orange, blanched split almonds to strew on top.

Beat the butter or margarine, and zest of orange, with the sugar to a cream. Then beat in the eggs one at a time. With the last of the eggs start adding the sifted flour to which the salt has already been sifted. Finally, add the prepared fruits and ground almonds.

Turn mixture into a prepared 20 cm (8") tin. Strew top with the blanched split almonds and bake in a moderate oven for approximately 2 hours at 180° C (350° F).

Note: If less eggs are used, compensate with one small teaspoon of baking powder.

Boiled Fruit Cake

$^1/_4$ teaspoon salt, 1 teaspoon baking powder, 2 tablespoons brandy, 2 beaten eggs, 2 cups flour, 1 teaspoon bicarbonate of soda, 1 cup raisins, 1 cup currants, 1 cup sultanas, 1 cup sugar, 125 g (4 oz) butter, 1 cup water, $^1/_2$ cup each of candied peel, nuts, dates, crystallised fruits and cherries.

Boil raisins, currants, sultanas, sugar and butter in the water for 20 minutes. Three minutes before the end of boiling time add the half cups of candied peel, nuts, dates, crystallised fruit and cherries. (The cherries and fruit should have been washed, dried and chopped.) Remove from the stove and while still warm, mix in the bicarbonate of soda. Cool and when quite cold, add the well-beaten eggs, sifted flour, baking powder and salt. Lastly add the brandy. Put into a 20 cm (8") tin and bake at 150° C (300° F) for one hour. Reduce the temperature to 130° C (250° F) and bake for a further 1–1$^1/_2$ hours.

✽   ✽   ✽

Raisins: Try plumping the raisins in brandy overnight before adding them to your fruit cake.

Preserves

It is not generally known, but South African women have earned a world-wide reputation for their bottled fruits, as well as for their preserves (and flower arrangements). From a Bloemfontein tombstone – of all places – we learn, among a list of attributes, that Mrs Jemima Cornelia Krause (wife of Dr Otto Krause) not only was awarded the First Prize in the O.F.S. Agricultural Show, 1892, for preserved fruit in bottles, but also a diploma of honour and a medal at the Centennial Columbian Exhibition, Chicago, U.S.A. 1892–93.

When one considers the small size of our White population, especially before the end of the last century, one realises just how high a standard our women set for themselves, and in so doing pioneered a field of preserving that is South Africa's own, namely for konfyt, as it was known – pieces of fruit suspended in syrup – as distinct from jam. But today the Afrikaans word *konfyt* covers whole and cut up preserves while *fynkonfyt* adequately covers pulped preserves, or jam.

Joey's Orange Preserve

Choose ripe firm navel oranges. Grate off the rind to remove most of the oil cells. Cut fruit in half and cover with cold water. Leave overnight. Throw water off but keep. Cover with fresh cold water and again leave overnight. This second water can be discarded.

Use 500 g (1 lb) sugar for 500 g (1 lb) fruit plus $^1/_2$ cup (125 ml) water. (The oranges will still be full of water from the soaking.) Measure off the sugar and water and boil until the sugar has melted. Gently place the orange halves in the syrup. Turn the heat high but as soon as it is boiling fast, lower the heat and let all cook gently for about 3 hours until the syrup thickens. Leave to cool. If the oranges are very juicy, they may not contain enough pectin for setting, then some pectin may be added – obtainable from the chemist or make your own. *(See Cookery in Southern Africa Traditional and Today.)* Spoon the halves gently into dry clean jars so as to make a good 'eye', i.e. the pieces not overlapping or crowded. Pour over the syrup. Seal with greaseproof paper or clingwrap before screwing on the lids.

✻   ✻   ✻

A test for genuine (natural) brown sugar. Pour warm water over a little of the sugar and leave for a while. If the sugar becomes white be assured it is not natural sugar but processed white sugar with a brown dye added to make it look attractive.

Preserving Whole Oranges for Show

An Old Prize-Winner's Instructions

Oranges can be packed one upon the other, or sideways, or they can be halved and packed to show the inside of the fruit, but should never be pressed out of shape. When packing, first pour in a little syrup, then one orange, add more syrup just to come up level with the orange, then add a second orange, and again syrup level with the orange; and go on until the bottle is full. See that the syrup covers the fruit completely; insert a knife, just slipping it in on one side of the bottle at the top, and allow the knife to lie in the fruit. This keeps the fruit under the syrup, and gives the syrup time to set and thicken, and the fruit to absorb the syrup. Next morning, when the knife is removed the fruit will not again rise to the top. Keep some syrup and re-fill the bottles next day. (The fruit must be completely covered, then closed air-tight.) Always cover the mouth of the bottle with a piece of butter muslin while pouring in the syrup; this will give a clearer syrup and remove all particles of fruit that may be floating in the syrup.

Mangoes in Syrup

Peel firm, ripe mangoes, pack them in jars, covering them with a syrup that has been made by boiling 155 g (5 oz) of sugar and 600 ml (1 pint) of water. Stand jars in a pan of water and simmer for 45 minutes. Fill up jars with boiling syrup again, then seal up.

Green Fig Preserve

Scrape unripe figs and cut a slit across the top (not too large). Lay them in a basin of water, to which has been added 2 tablespoons of lime. (This quantity is for 100 figs.) Lay a plate, with a weight on it, on top of the figs, or they will float on the water. After they have soaked for about 12 hours, take them out and wash them until clean. Have ready a saucepan in which you have put about 3.8 litres (3 quarts) of clean water, one teaspoon of bicarbonate of soda and one tablespoon of salt. Allow the figs to boil up in this, taking care to leave the lid off the saucepan. When soft enough to be easily pierced with a reed or a toothpick, take them out and drain through a colander, or on a cloth.

Take 1 kg (2 lb) sugar *more* than the weight of the fruit. Make a clear syrup (1 cup of water to 1 cup of sugar). When strained and cooled, lay the figs in it for a night. The next day, cook the fruit on a slow heat until it is quite clear – 3–4 hours. Place the figs and syrup in small jars and seal.

Note: Before scraping the figs it is a good idea to wrap your fingers in elastoplast, to prevent the acid from making them raw.

Sour Fig Konfyt

Suurvyekonfyt

Top 1 kg (2 lb) of sour figs and wash them well. Put them in a basin of lightly salted water to soak overnight. The following morning wash them again. Then boil together 750 g (1$^1/_2$ lb) sugar, a piece of stick cinnamon and 900 ml (1$^1/_2$ pints) of water. When the syrup has boiled for a few minutes, add the fruit and cook it gently until the fruit is soft and the sugar thick. Do not add any water. Bottle while hot in sterilised jars.

Grapefruit Preserve

Skins Only

Why throw away the skin of your grapefruit? Using the skins, you can have a delicious preserve for the cost of the sugar only. After the inside of the halved fruit has been eaten, carefully remove and throw away the white pith on the inside of each half. Collect the skins and keep them in the refrigerator until you have sufficient to make a batch of preserve.

Place the skins in a salt solution (1 dessertspoon of salt to 1 .25 litres (2 pints) of cold water). Slightly grate the skins all over, then wash, and put them back into the salt water again. Repeat this process of soaking and washing once more, removing the skins the next day. Wash again, then boil in fresh water for $^1/_4$ hour. Repeat this process 3 times, to remove bitterness, and until the fruit is soft and transparent. Weigh it, and make a syrup from 500 g (1 lb) granulated sugar for each 500 g (1 lb) of fruit, with 2 cups of water for each 500 g (1 lb). Bring the syrup to the boil, then add the fruit. Cook on medium heat for $1^1/_4$–$1^1/_2$ hours. Bubbles appear all over the surface just before it is ready.

How to Test: When cooked, the spoon will stick to a dry saucer. Bottle the preserve while hot, in sterilised bottles.

Points for Preserving

Sugar: For bottling jams, jellies and marmalade use granulated sugar. For chutneys use brown sugar, according to taste.

Reducing the Liquid: When making jams and marmalades, the fruit mixture in the pan should be reduced by about $^1/_3$ before the sugar is added, to give the correct proportion of water to sugar in the finished preserve. *Always use sterilised jars for preserving.*

Green Grape Jam

Western Province Farm Recipe

When grapes will not ripen on the vines, they can be made into very nice jam as follows: Pick them from the stalks and wash well. Place in a copper or enamel preserving pan with cold water to cover and boil till the seeds come away from the grapes. Pass through a sieve to remove skins and seeds. Measure the pulp, and to every 600 ml (1 pint) of this add 500 g (1 lb) sugar or a little more if the grapes are very green. Place again in the pan after the bottom has been oiled with a little salad oil or fresh butter. Return to the fire and boil together for $^1/_2$ hour until it jellies when a little is tested on a plate. Pour into bottles and set aside until quite cold. Screw on the tops and store.

Carrot Marmalade

2 oranges, 1 cup water, 3 cups grated carrots, 4 cups sugar, 1 small piece ginger root, juice from 3 lemons, $^1/_2$ teaspoon salt.

Wash and peel oranges. Mince in a food grinder. Cook in 1 cup water until tender. Put grated carrots through the food grinder; then cook in a small amount of water until tender. Drain well. Blend sugar, hot carrots, ginger, orange pulp, orange peel, lemon juice and salt. Boil gently, stirring frequently, until marmalade is thick and very syrupy. Ladle immediately into hot jelly or canning jars. Fill to within 3 mm ($^1/_8$″) of top. Screw cap on evenly and tightly. Invert for a few seconds and stand jars upright to cool.

Variations: rhubarb, prunes or three slices of drained pineapple may be substituted for the oranges.

Loquat Jelly

Wash the loquats, cut off the rough ends and stalks and remove the stones. Boil the loquats in water, sufficient to flood them, till reduced to a pulp; strain off the juice and add an equal weight of granulated sugar. Boil till it 'jells' when tested on a cold plate.

Cape Gooseberry Jam

Sorry to disillusion some of our readers but actually the Cape gooseberry is not advertising the Cape Province. The 'cape' derives from the shawl or cape which cocoons the fruit.

Wash berries, prick with darning needle. Allow 500 g (1 lb) of sugar to 500 g (1 lb) fruit. Bring water to boil (1 cup to 3 cups fruit). Add fruit. Boil till berries can be easily pierced with needle. Now add sugar warmed up in oven. Skim constantly and boil to the right consistency. Stir occasionally to prevent burning. This should 'jell' beautifully when tested on saucer. Put in sterilised bottles and leave overnight. Next morning, put greaseproof paper dipped in brandy on jam, before closing bottles.

Amatingulu Jelly

This South Coast 'plum' is far better than cranberry jelly with meats.

Wash Amatingulu fruit thoroughly, then place in large pan with a small amount of water. Boil steadily and fairly fast until the fruit is very soft and the liquid somewhat thick. This takes about three hours. Sieve through butter muslin, allowing plenty of time. Measure cup for cup of white sugar, bring to the boil and boil steadily and slowly for about 20 minutes until the jelly drops very sluggishly from the end of a spoon. Pour into jars and seal.

The thick part remaining on the sieve forms an excellent kitchen jam with sugar added.

Vegetable Marrow Jam

3 kg (6 lb) marrow (young ones), 3 kg (6 lb) sugar, 3 lemons, 60 g (2 oz) whole ginger.

Peel and core marrow. The marrows must be still quite young. Cut into dice, put on a flat dish covered with sugar, and allow to stand for 24 hours. Then pare 2 lemons thinly and add the rind and strained juice of 3 lemons to the fruit and also bruise whole ginger tied up in muslin, and add. Put all together in a preserving pan and boil for 1$^1/_2$ hours, skimming well. Take out the lemon rind and ginger. The marrow will now be quite tender and transparent. A wineglassful of whisky or cooking brandy added just before the jam is done, is a great improvement.

When cold ladle into jars, cover well and store.

Papaw Jam

2 papaws ($^1/_2$ ripe), 250 g ($^1/_2$ lb) sugar, 2 lemons, 125 g (4 oz) whole ginger.

Take 2 medium-sized half-ripe papaws. Cut into pieces and allow to stand overnight with sugar sprinkled over them. Cut up 2 large lemons and soak all night in 600 ml (1 pint) of water. Next day boil the lemons till tender then pour over the papaws. Add the whole ginger smashed up with a hammer, and boil until all the papaw is tender. Weigh and add 375 g ($^3/_4$ lb) sugar to every 500 g (1 lb) or jam. Boil till it jellies when tried on a saucer. Bottle when nearly cold.

Sliced Peach Jam

Perskesnippers

Peel and slice peaches thinly. Wash in strong salt water. Allow 375 g ($^3/_4$ lb) sugar to 500 g (1 lb) sliced peaches and 1 cup of water to every 500 g (1 lb) of fruit. Bring the water to the boil, add the fruit. Cook the fruit until tender. Now add the sugar which has been warmed up in the oven. (This is done so that the sugar can dissolve readily in the jam.) A piece of bruised ginger added to the fruit improves the flavour. Boil to the right consistency (testing frequently on a saucer). Skim jam – if necessary – without stirring. Put in sterilized bottles and leave overnight. Next morning cover jam with grease-proof paper dipped in brandy, just before closing the bottles.

Orange Peel

Always use only the peel from sweet oranges. Take any quantity of peel, and remove as much white pith as possible from the inside, then cut the peel into 5 mm ($^1/_4''$) strips. Place the peel in a pan, cover with cold water and bring slowly to the boil. Drain off the water, add fresh and reboil. Repeat this process 2 or 3 times. Cool the peel, weigh and place it in a pan, adding to it an equal amount of granulated sugar. Just cover this with water, bring to the boil slowly, to dissolve the sugar, and cook gently until the peel is tender and clear. Strain, and then toss the peel in granulated sugar. Keep in a warm place to dry. Then roll the peel in sugar again, and store in a screw-top jar. If you wish to use this peel in cakes, wash off all the sugary coating first, otherwise it will sink to the bottom of the cake.

Spiced Crab Apples

A Silwood Speciality

3 kg (6 lb) crab apples, 2–3 strips lemon peel, 425 ml ($^3/_4$ pint) wine vinegar, 1–2 whole cloves, 900 ml ($1^1/_2$ pints) water, 500 g (1 lb) sugar, 1 stick cinnamon, 3 peppercorns.

Wash and trim the crab apples, then simmer them in the water with the lemon peel until just tender; remove from the heat. Place the sugar and vinegar in a pan and add 900 ml ($1^1/_2$ pints) of the liquid from the fruit. Tie the spices in a muslin bag and add to the liquid. Bring to the boil slowly, to dissolve the sugar, and boil for 1 minute. Remove the pan from the heat and add the crab apples. Simmer gently until the syrup has reduced to a coating consistency, 30–40 minutes. Remove the bag of spices after the first $^1/_2$ hour. Place the fruit in small jars, cover with syrup and cover as for jam.

Silwood's Crab Apple Cheese

Clean the apples, and cut away all damaged parts with a silver knife.

Put in a light, covered earthenware jar, and cook in the oven till tender enough to squeeze through a coarse cheese cloth. Allow 375 g ($^3/_4$ lb) of pulp, put in a preserving pan and boil for an hour, skimming through. Put into fancy moulds, and cover.

Lemon Cheese
Suurlemoenbotter

Lemon cheese and lemon curd, in the strict English meaning, had nothing to do with cheese, being lemon-flavoured butter, with eggs added. The Afrikaans *suurlemoenbotter* is actually a more explicit description for it is a 'butter', eggs added. As lemon cheese utilised dairy products it was made on English and Boer farms and the lemon cheese tartlets were served with coffee or tea as a special treat. We wonder why lemon cheese is so seldom seen on our tables today.

Lemon Curd
Green If You Wish

At the Feast of the Orange Leaves Malays usually serve delicious little sponge cakes topped with green and lemon curd and decorated with whipped cream. To make the green curd, add green vegetable colouring to the lemon curd.

2 cups granulated sugar, 4 large lemons, 5 eggs, $^1/_2$ cup butter.

Wash and dry the lemons carefully, grate the rind thinly, squeeze out all the juice. Put juice, rind, beaten eggs, butter and sugar into the top of a double boiler. Heat the mixture, stirring well with a wooden spoon until the sugar dissolves and the curd thickens. Remove the pan from the heat, strain curd into hot sterilised jars and cover at once.

Rose Petal Conserve

Red rose petals, sugar, orange flower water.

Red roses make the best conserve and they must be gathered when fully open but before they begin to fade. Cut off the white heels, for these have a bitter flavour. Dry the petals on sieves out of direct sunlight and, if possible, in a draught as then they dry quickly. When dried put 500 g (1 lb) of petals into a muslin bag and plunge for a moment into boiling water. Drain well. Have ready a syrup made with 500 g (1 lb) of loaf sugar and very little water. Add 2 tablespoons of orange flower water. Put in the petals and cook until the conserve is very thick. Keep on pressing the petals under the syrup. Pour into small jars and cover down securely as for jam. The more richly scented the roses the better the flavour.

How to Frost Fruits

Enhance ordinary small fruits by giving them a frosty, fairy-like appearance by brushing them with egg white, then cover with castor sugar and leave in a warm place to dry.

To Frost Holly-Leaves

An Old English Method

Take some holly-leaves, cleanse them thoroughly, lay them on a large dish some little distance from the fire, and let them remain there until perfectly dry. Dip them into butter, melted until it will run, strew white powdered sugar over them, and dry them before the fire. Keep in a dry place until wanted for use.

Crystallised Rose Leaves

500 g (1 lb) rose leaves, 500 g (1 lb) granulated sugar, white of an egg.

Wash the rose leaves, make a syrup of the sugar and 600 ml (1 pint) water, and add the white of egg well whisked. Remove the scum as it rises, and when the syrup is quite clear and rather thick, add the rose leaves and cook slowly for about an hour.

Crystallised Kumquats

Japanese Oranges

Wash the kumquats carefully and cook in boiling water till tender and transparent. Let them drain and then make a syrup in the proportion of twice as much sugar as water, letting it boil till it spins a heavy thread. Put in the fruit and boil for 10 minutes, drain and roll each in granulated sugar; leave on a wire sieve till quite dry.

✢   ✢   ✢

Sugared Flowers

Made at Silwood Kitchen, Grannies' Way

This is a very easy way of preserving small flowers for cakes and sweets – enchanting with their delicate frosted colourings and edible, of course. They store well, too.

Choose small flowers without solid centres; petals by themselves are most suitable. There is a wonderful variety from which to make your selection: sprigs of fresh, green mint, single wallflowers, tiny sprays of forget-me-not, rambler rose petals or baby roses, violets, violas and pansies. All these are pretty and easy to sugar.

Beat an egg white with a tablespoon of white wine or cold water until they are *just* mixed. Have ready a piece of greaseproof paper sprinkled with castor sugar. Pick the flowers, which must be absolutely fresh, and do not wash them, but brush them with a fine brush. Now, using an artist's paint brush, lightly coat the petals with the egg-white mixture, being careful to cover the whole surface, not thickly but evenly. Then lay the flowers in sugar, and sprinkle the sugar lightly over each flower until it is evenly coated. Lay your sugared flowers on a tray, and put it in a dry, airy place, to allow them to dry naturally. (You can place them in a cool oven, but the colour is preserved better if they are dried in the air.)

When the flowers are crisp and thoroughly dry, they are ready for storing. Allow about 2 or 3 days before storing them.

Favoured Sugars

For a distinctive flavouring for cakes and puddings – like granny made – we offer you these delectable sugars.

Our Special Flavoured Sugar

Place 2 vanilla pods (obtainable from most large supermarkets) in a honey jar, and cover with granulated sugar. Add the grated rind of an orange and a tablespoon of brandy. Put the lid on, seal, shake well and store. After a few days, this sugar is ready for use, as a flavouring for cakes and puddings. Keep topping up with sugar, rind and a little brandy as you use it. Superb to use, it adds a wonderful new flavour to your favourite recipes. Actually, we use a honey jar for the measurement and then transfer it to an air-tight container.

Vanilla Sugar

Half fill a screw-top jar with sugar, add 3 or 4 vanilla pods or beans (obtainable from large supermarkets). Always use this sugar when making puddings, in preference to vanilla essence and sugar. Top up the jar at intervals with sugar (as the pods last a long time), and keep it tightly closed.

Citrus Sugar

Simply wash and dry oranges and/or lemons. Using a fine grater, grate the skins (no pith), and then sprinkle them with granulated sugar. Leave the mixture in a warm, dry place and stir well at intervals, each time sprinkling with a little more sugar. Continue thus until the moisture has been absorbed by the successive sprinklings, and the top surface is dry. Store the flavouring in an air-tight jar, to use as required.

Cinnamon Sugar

Take 30 g (1 oz) of ground cinnamon and mix with 185 g (6 oz) of sugar. Bottle and use as required.

How to Colour Sugar

Place some granulated sugar in a basin, add a drop or two of vegetable colouring and rub well between the fingers until it is uniform in colour. Place, spread out, on a baking tray in a warm place to dry out, then put in an air-tight jar to store.

Zest Sugar Cubes

Zest, an ingredient often mentioned in cookery, is the name given to the oil in the skins of all citrus fruits which gives them their characteristic smell. Here's an old hint: Before peeling oranges, lemons or naartjies wash and dry them well, then rub sugar cubes all over the skin until they are soaked with zest. Store the cubes in an air-tight jar and add to milk puddings, etc., instead of ordinary sugar.

Brandied Fruits

Our Time-Honoured Method

To the French Huguenots we owe not only our wine industry, but also our knowledge of preserved and brandied fruits.

To prepare brandied fruits correctly at home, the various fruits must be perfect – just ripe, which means firm to the touch, of best quality, of good colour and without blemish; thus the full aroma and flavour will be retained. The best results are obtained by preserving the fruit in glass jars. The larger fruits should be blanched (dipped into boiling water) while others may be put directly into the alcohol. You can brandy a single type of fruit, or a mixture of various kinds, such as plums, peaches, apricots or grapes.

Cut in half firm, unblemished peaches, plums, apricots. Prick grapes 2 or 3 times with a needle. Take an equal weight of sugar and fruit, and layer in preserving jar until ³/₄ full. Pour in enough *Oude Meester* liqueur brandy to cover, seal and allow to stand for at least a month before using.

Brandied Peaches

Wash 12 ripe firm peaches, scald in boiling water to cover. Remove and plunge into cold water. Now remove peels and return peaches and 500 g (1 lb) golden brown sugar to the boiling water. Simmer till tender (about 10 minutes). Remove fruit from syrup and put in a sterilised jar. Pour over its own syrup and 1 .2 litres (1 quart) liqueur brandy. Seal lid with melted candle grease. Allow to ripen 1 month before use.

Brandied Pineapple

1 large can of pineapple pieces, 3 cloves, 5 cm (2″) stick of cinnamon, ¹/₂ cup, (¹/₄ pint) brandy or kirsch.

Drain the juice from the pineapple and put into a saucepan; add the cloves and cinnamon and simmer gently together until of a syrupy consistency. Add the pineapple pieces and simmer them for a further 10 minutes. Remove from the heat and add the brandy or kirsch. Cool, then pack the fruit into a wide-necked bottle. Pour on the syrup and seal.

Brandied Grapes

Put fine, firm, whole and perfect grapes into jars, without filling them too full. Cover with liqueur brandy, and allow to macerate for 3 weeks. Then finish by filling the jars with cold syrup made with 500 g (1 lb) granulated sugar to 1 cup water. Shake the jars to mix well.

Brandied Cherries

Though not so traditional, this recipe is simple to prepare. Put ripe cherries into jars and add 155 g (5 oz) castor sugar per 500 g (1 lb) cherries.

Cover with liqueur brandy, seal airtight, and allow to macerate for 5–6 weeks. A vanilla pod and cinnamon stick should also be included.

Brandied Apricots or Figs

Put apricots into a wide-mouthed jar, sprinkling sugar between each layer in the proportion of 500 g (1 lb) apricots to 250 g ($^1/_2$ lb) sugar. Fill the jar with brandy and cook in a saucepan of water until the brandy begins to simmer. Remove the apricots and pack them in jars. Pour the syrup into the jars and when cold, screw on lids.

If using figs, add a little lemon juice.

Lemon Brandy

For Flavouring Custards

Take the thin rind of 6 fresh lemons, and put them in a bottle with 600 ml (1 pint) of brandy. Let them infuse for 6 weeks, then strain the liquid, and put it in small bottles, cork and seal securely, and put aside for use.

✻   ✻   ✻

Melons . . . Traditional Fruit

But When is a Melon Ripe?

Among our galaxy of traditional fruits are the problem fruits like melons – because we are not always sure when they are ripe. The watermelon, with its greeny satin skin and vivid pink interior, has for generations been a traditional favourite for parties and at Christmas time, one melon feeding the whole family and providing plenty of konfyt from the skin throughout the year. As children, all remember Dad buying watermelons from the hawker, lifting them, one by one on to his head, to hear the "crack." A ripe watermelon should sound hollow when thumped with the knuckle. If ripe the skin will peel easily.

Spanspek and canteloupe melons should be chosen by their fragrance; sniff them as you do an apple. The winter melon or honeydew is the pale green smooth variety. To test for ripeness press on the end which joins the stem and if it feels soft it is probably a good one.

Personally, we don't agree that melon should be added to fruit salad, as quite often the peculiar flavour drowns that of other fruits. Melon is best served cubed or balled and a mixture of melon varieties can be delicious. Lemon juice and sugar and ground ginger bring out the flavour of melon. In addition to the family 'ear to to ear' slices or eaten with the formality of a dessert knife and fork, here is a way of serving any type of melon.

Watermelon Compote

Watermelon balls, using small scoop or cut into small squares (about 6 cups), $^1/_2$ cup castor sugar, 1 cup sherry.

Place prepared melon in a glass bowl, add sugar and toss gently until dissolved. Add the sherry; toss again and chill before serving.

Malay Sweetmeats

Mebos is one of the oldest Cape 'sweets'. Whenever the old Cape farmers had a bumper apricot harvest much of the fruit was preserved for the winter months. A method of drying apricots was to rub them with salt and spread them on the roofs to soften in the sun. After three days the family was rounded up to help 'squeeze' the pips from the fruit which was later put back on the roof to dry out thoroughly.

Mebos Sweets

500 g (1 lb) dried apricots, 1 kg (2 lb) granulated sugar, 3 tablespoons water.

Soak the apricots overnight with sufficient water to cover. Drain them well, then put through the mincer twice. Put the minced apricots into a saucepan with the sugar and 3 tablespoons water. Boil until thick and until the mixture leaves the sides of the pan, stir all the time. Pour into a greased pan to set until hard, then cut into squares and roll in castor sugar.

Peach Sweets

An Old Farm Recipe

Peel and mince the fruit. Clingstone peaches should first be boiled soft in a small quantity of water. Press the fruit through a sieve, and add ¹/₂ cup sugar to every cup of fruit pulp; cook until the mixture is thick and comes away from the sides of the saucepan; keep stirring, to prevent burning; pour out on a greased board, marble slab or stone table, and spread out in layers 12 mm (¹/₂″) thick; allow to dry out for 3 to 4 days, or until it is quite stiff and no longer sticky; cut into desired shapes, and roll in sugar. Allow to dry for another 2 or 3 days, and pack in bottles or between waxed sheets in wooden boxes.

Fruit Rolls

Truly Traditional Sweetmeats

All kinds of fresh fruits may be used. In the case of hard fruits, such as quinces, apples, cling-stone peaches, etc., it is necessary to boil the fruits first in very little water, until tender, but not mushy. Drain through a sieve, and when cold, mince. Sweeten according to taste: one cup granulated sugar to 1 cup pulp and ¹/₈ teaspoon salt. Mix well, and add a little vanilla essence to taste.

Take sheets of brown paper, grease well with a little soft butter, and spread the fruit evenly over the paper to about 6 mm(¹/₄″) thick. Put in the sun to dry. This takes about 12 hours. Just before it is quite dry, it should be loosened at the edges of the paper, using a knife. Leave a little longer till quite dry. Sprinkle well with granulated sugar and roll up like a Swiss roll.

In the case of soft fruits, such as apricots, peaches and figs, they should not be boiled, merely minced, sweetened and treated as above.

Malay hawker, Cape Town, 19th century.

Quince Smear

From a Farmer's Wife

Peel and core as many quinces as you require, mince and add a little water. Boil until quite soft and very thick indeed. Weigh and add an equal weight of sugar, return to the pan and boil (stirring constantly, as it is very liable to burn), until sugar is dissolved. The 'smear' must be very thick, as otherwise it takes too long to dry. Butter freely large meat dishes or clean boards, and when it is cold spread the mixture about 12 mm ($^1/_2$'') thick on them. Leave in a cool, airy place to dry out for a few days. Sprinkle freely with sugar and roll up. The rolls may be rolled in sugar and stored in air-tight tins lined with grease-proof paper.

Tameletjies

These sweetmeats were sold by the Malay vendors 50 years ago in the streets of Cape Town. Today, sad to say, they are only made by the women to serve at their Malay special feasts. Two varieties of tameletjies are given here. One is *pitjie tameletjie* and the other *ertjie tameletjie*.

2 cups sugar and 1 cup of water are boiled to a caramel at 180° C (350° F) (or until it froths). Clarify with the white of an egg. While boiling briskly, add dennepitte (pine kernels) or almonds, grated lemon, naartjie peel or petals of orange blossoms. Turn into well-buttered pan and mark into little squares. Cool before serving.

Pitjie Tameletjie

Pine Kernel Toffee

2 cups dennepitte (pine kernels), 1 tablespoon butter, 2 pieces of dried ginger, 4 cups sugar, 2 cups water.

Boil sugar, butter and water and ginger until brown and sugar boiling. Add the dennepitte. Stir well and drop in little mounds on small squares of greased greaseproof paper. When set and cold, screw ends to keep the moisture out.

Ertjies Tameletjie

Dried Pea Toffee (Coon's Candy)

When the pine kernels are not available the Malays substitute dried peas. Soak 2 cups of dried peas in sufficient water to cover overnight. Next day parboil peas for a few minutes. Drain well. Now make the toffee.

4 cups sugar, 2 cups water, 1 tablespoon butter, a few pieces of dry ginger.

Boil all together until the mixture is brown. Add the prepared *ertjies,* stir well and set in little mounds in squares of grease paper. When set and cold wrap them up tight to keep the moisture out.

Index

𝔉arewell

After 10 years of arduous but fruitful service at the Cape, Maria, Jan and their six children set sail in the *Mars* for Batavia. It is recorded that Jan never saw his dear Holland again, as he died in the East. One of his sons, Abraham, second European child to be born at the Cape, grew up in the service of the Dutch East India Company to become Viceroy of the East Indies

Other Books by Lesley Faull and Vida Heard

Cookery in Southern Africa Traditional and Today
ABC for Cooks

Cordons Bleus Books by Lesley Faull
edited by Vida Heard

Braai and Barbecue in Southern Africa (3rd edition)
Meat on the Menu
Rice Recipes and Curries
Bread Buns Cakes and Cookies

✻   ✻   ✻

By Lesley Faull in collaboration with Cordon Bleu
(Britain) Muriel Downes and Rosemary Hume

Fynkookkuns (52 weeklies)
Onthaal met Fynkookkuns
Keurige Vleis met Fynkookkuns
Kook Gerus met Fynkookkuns

✻   ✻   ✻

By Lesley Faull

Party Fare (3rd edition)
Their Secret was Sugar
Hul Geheim was Suiker
Inspired By Sugar
Met Suiker as Spoorslag
Milk Makes It
Melk Maak Dit

Soft Covers by Lesley Faull

Cream Makes the Difference
Buttermilk Recipes

Brenda Lighton